HOW TO MAKE ANYONE FALL IN LOVE WITH YOU

How to Make Anyone Fall in Love with You

LEIL LOWNDES

Thorsons

Thorsons
An Imprint of HarperCollins*Publishers*
77–85 Fulham Palace Road,
Hammersmith, London W6 8JB

First published by Contemporary Books, an Imprint of NTC/
Contemporary Publishing Company, Illinois, USA
Published by Thorsons, London 1997
11.12.13.14.15.16.17.18.19.20

A catalogue record for this book
is available from the British Library

ISBN 0 7225 3470 1

Printed and bound in Great Britain by
Clays Ltd, St Ives plc

To fulfil the promise of the title, *How to Make Anyone Fall in Love with You* offers 85 techniques based on scientific studies into the nature of romantic love.

Contents

Chapter One

Anyone? Yes, Practically Anyone

'I don't understand. I'm attractive, intelligent, sensitive, accomplished. Why doesn't he or she fall for me? Why can't I find love?' How many times have you beaten your fists on the pillow asking yourself this question?

You open this book sceptically, yet harbouring hope, for the solution. You read the title: *How to Make Anyone Fall in Love with You.*

'That's a big promise.' you say. Indeed, it is. But the promise of this book is yours if you are willing to follow a scientifically sound plan to capture the heart of a Potential Love Partner.

Why, when history is strewn with broken hearts, do we now claim the means to make someone fall in love with us? Because, after centuries of resistance, science is finally unravelling what romantic love actually is, what triggers it, what kills it, and what makes it last.

Just as ancient tribesmen saw an eclipse and thought it was black magic, we looked at love and thought it was enchantment. Sometimes, especially during those first blissful moments when we want to stop strangers on the street and cry out, 'I'm in love!' it may feel like enchantment, but, as we enter the 21st century, we are discovering that love is a definable and calculated blend of chemistry, biology, and psychology. (And, well, maybe a *little* black magic thrown in.)

As science sets sail in previously unknown seas, we are at last beginning to understand the rudiments of that 'most insane, most delusive, and most transient of passions', as George Bernard Shaw described love. And what makes people want to stay in that 'excited, abnormal, and exhausting condition continuously until death do them part'? The question, and the quandary, of 'Precisely what is love?' is not new. It is one that has been given serious consideration throughout the ages by cerebral heavyweights like Plato, Sigmund Freud, and Charlie Brown.

In the darkened Broadway theatre in 1950, the audiences of *South Pacific* were in total harmony with Ezio Pinza when he pondered, 'Who can explain it? Who can tell you why? Fools give you reasons. Wise men never try.' Well, recently, many wise men and women *have* tried, and succeeded. Don't blame Rodgers and Hammerstein. When they were composing romantic musicals, the scientific community was as perplexed about love as Nellie and Emile de Bacque singing their bewilderment about some enchanted evening.

 ## Science 'Discovers' Sex

Long before Sigmund Freud tackled the subject, analytical scientific minds agreed that love was basic to the human experience. But their rational brains also deemed that evaluating, classifying, and defining romantic love was impossible and therefore a waste of time and money. Freud went to his deathbed declaring, 'We really know very little about love.'

His dying words remained the scientific doctrine. At least until the early 1970s when a pioneer-spirited band of social psychologists took up the scientists' constant cries of *why*?

and *how*? They began asking themselves – and everybody they could lure into their laboratories – questions about romantic love.

Two women psychologists made a breakthrough by inadvertently focusing the attention of the modern press on the ancient question of 'What is love?' Ellen Berscheid, PhD, with a colleague, Elaine Hatfield, managed to wangle an $84,000 federal grant to study romantic love. Berscheid convinced the National Science Foundation to open its coffers by declaring, 'We already understand the mating habits of the stickleback fish. It is time to turn to a new species.'

Berscheid's study, like others before, might have gone unnoticed and unpublished, except for a dozen or so pages in an obscure professional journal. Fortunately for love seekers everywhere, one morning on Capitol Hill, former United States Senator William Proxmire of Wisconsin was going through his papers. Buried deep in the pile was the NSF's 'frivolous' grant to two women to study relationships.

Proxmire hit the dome! Eighty-four thousand dollars to study *what*? He dashed off an explosive press release announcement that romantic love was not a science and, furthermore, he roared, 'National Science Foundation, get out of the love racket. Leave that to Elizabeth Barrett Browning and Irving Berlin.' Proxmire then added a personal note: 'I'm also against it because I don't *want* the answer.' He assumed everyone felt the same. How wrong he was!

Proxmire's reaction set off an international firestorm that raged around Berscheid for the next two years. 'Extra! Extra! Read all about it. *National Science Foundation Tackles Love!*' Newspapers had a field day. Cameras and microphones zeroed in on Berscheid with gusto. The quiet researcher's office was swamped with mail.

Proxmire's potshot at love had backfired. Instead of putting an end to the 'frivolous pursuit', his brouhaha generated tempestuous interest in the study of love. James Reston of the *New*

York Times declared that if Berscheid et al. could find 'the answer to our pattern of romantic love, marriage, disillusion, divorce – and the children left behind – it would be the best investment of federal money since Jefferson made the Louisiana Purchase.'

It was as though Ellen Berscheid had pulled her finger out of the dyke. Ever since, there has been a torrent of studies scrutinizing every aspect of love. Respected social scientists with names like Foa, Murstein, Dion, Aron, Rubin, and many others relatively unknown outside the scientific world have given us an as-yet-unopened gift – a gift we will unwrap now: the results of their labours, their studies, teach us (although that was not their purpose) how to make somebody fall in love.

Granted, some of the studies do not guide us directly to that goal. To find the relevant studies, I had to comb through hundreds of scientific probings with cumbersome titles such as 'The Implications of Exchange Orientation on the Dyadic Functioning of Heterosexual Cohabitors', (What?) Some studies had mice listening to classical music, then jazz and blues, to see which made them hornier.[1] Other studies which were worthless to our goal explored sexual attraction to corpses,[2] and then there were studies on tantric motionless intercourse,[3] which, I assumed, works only when a couple's honeymoon cruise ship hits rocky seas.

Happily, many studies bore tastier and more practical fruit. Especially helpful were studies by an intrepid researcher named Timothy Perper, a PhD student who spent many hours observing subjects in his favourite laboratory, called a 'singles' bar'. We also benefit from brilliant examinations by Robert Sternberg and his colleagues who explored theories of love. We learn from insightful early explorations into the elements of infatuation by Dorothy Tennov and others. There were courageous, if relatively unknown, researchers like Carol Ronai. She actually took a job as a table dancer in a topless bar to record what facial expressions turn men on.[4]

How More Research Was Compiled

My own firsthand research, although less daring, was no less vigorous. For more than ten years, before becoming a communications consultant and trainer, I was director of a research group I founded called The Project.

The Project was a New York City-based not-for-profit corporation established to explore sexuality and relationships. During my tenure with The Project, I interviewed and catalogued thousands of subjects on what they sought in a partner. I gathered information from the students at the dozens of universities where I was invited to speak on my research.

Like the work of researcher Ellen Berscheid, The Project experienced an unsought avalanche of attention which brought it to national attention. A *Time* magazine reporter covered one of our sessions and wrote a full-page article declaring 'Sex Fantasy Goes to Broadway', which, indeed, it did.

One arm of The Project had volunteers presenting psychodramatizations of their actual love fantasies on stage. Because there was no nudity and no explicit language, the squeaky-clean dramatizations were unique and caught the attention of the three major television networks, which presented excerpts of the vignettes on national programmes. This, in turn, spawned dozens of articles in respected mainstream publications in America and Europe.

As a result, people from all over the world sent us their stories, their fantasies, their longings for love. They called or wrote to The Project detailing precisely what they sought in a romantic partner. Most of the letters and calls we received were prefaced with comments like, 'I've never told anyone but ...' The callers and writers then proceeded to dilvulge their deepest desires to the anonymous Project. We listened, gratefully, as we gathered data on what made, or would make, people fall in love.

How the Techniques Were Developed

Let us leave the world of sexuality for a moment. Come with me to my second discipline, the field of communications. It is here I take the findings, and turn them into workable techniques to make someone fall in love with you.

It has been proved beyond any doubt that there are ways to induce desired behaviour from people. If there were not, all psychologists and thousands of corporate trainers, myself included, would be out of business. There are established methods for invoking various emotions and for changing people's behaviour. For example, we can learn how to deal with difficult people or how to make troublesome employees respond in the desired way.

Feedback from seminars I have presented for government organizations, universities, professional associations, and corporations convinces me that we can indeed effect changes in behaviour patterns. We accomplish this complex task by first understanding people's basic needs and motivations, then by employing the right verbal and nonverbal skills to modify their behaviour.

That is what I do in this book. Drawing from the scientific studies, I reveal the basic needs and motivations that make someone fall in love. Then I give you the right verbal and nonverbal skills to induce the behaviour you want – in this case, to make that person fall in love with you.

This book is the result of many years of research and exploration into several disciplines: interpersonal relationships, human sexuality, communication skills, and gender differences. We not only draw from scientific studies into the nature of love and from my personal research, but we also benefit from the work of modern therapists and communications analysts. I am especially grateful for the work of sociolinguist Deborah Tannen[5] and the clever Mars/Venus analogies of therapist John Gray,[6] who made it common knowledge that men and women have vastly different styles of thinking and communicating.

What is the recipe for making someone fall in love with you? Can it be reduced to a formula? The following sounds simple, but it is actually quite complicated.

You start with a solid scientific base of what makes up inter-personal attraction. Then you gather profound information about your *Quarry* (the person you want to make fall in love with you). Next, you employ sophisticated, often subliminal, communication techniques to meet his or her conscious and subconscious needs. Finally, you secure your Quarry with your spicy perception of *precisely* what he or she wants sexually. There you have it: the formula for making a Potential Love Partner fall in love with you.

 ## How I Tested the Techniques

I was not content with simply relying on research. I needed to see if these techniques would work in the field. Several years ago, to test my theories, I created a seminar with the same title as this book, 'How to Make Anyone Fall in Love with You'.

Invitations flowed in from all over the country from colleges, singles' groups, clubs, and continuing education organizations. It is on this playing field that the material has been tested. And the feedback from my students is, 'Yes!' You can make someone fall in love with you.

Is it a simple task? No.

Does it require sacrifice? Yes.

You may decide, after reading this book, that capturing his or her heart is simply not worth having to give that much of yourself. But if you do want to proceed, follow me. We will explore the skills needed to accomplish the task, to make the Potential Love Partner of your choice fall in love with you. (You notice that I have used the words *Potential Love Partner* several times. I will do so throughout the book because, although it is bulkier, the phrase is more accurate than *anyone*, which my publisher wisely decided is more readable.)

Who are your Potential Love Partners? Firstly, a Potential Love Partner (or *PLP*) is *anyone* who is ready for love. Timing, if not everything, at least counts a lot. For example, if someone has just lost a beloved spouse, he or she may not be ready for love. That knocks him or her – temporarily – out of the PLP category.

Secondly, a Potential Love Partner is *anyone* free of esoteric psychological (or *Lovemap*) needs. These are needs that, through no fault of your own, you cannot fulfil. We will talk a lot about your Quarry's Lovemap later.

That leaves many Potential Love Partners, a myriad of hearts to choose from. Let us embark now upon the path that leads you to the heart of the man or woman you desire.

Chapter Two

What Makes People Fall in Love?

The Six Elements

What are the long-awaited results of Berscheid's early studies and the deluge of those that followed? Well, maybe Freud was right. Romantic love *is* enigmatic. It is difficult to capture and convert into computerized, controlled bits and bytes of information. Instead, treating it as if it were a virus, scholars are tackling specific questions about love, nailing down a few facets at a time. They have made tremendous progress.

Out of the cascade of studies, six verities emerge about what makes people fall in love. To be a successful Hunter or Huntress of hearts, you must, like Cupid, be a skilful archer, and aim your arrow dead centre at the following six targets.

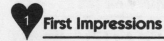

1 First Impressions

You Never Get a Second Chance at Love at First Sight

The first moments you spot your Quarry – and he or she gets a glimpse of you – can be decisive. Herein lies a 'go/no go' decision. Scientists tell us that love's seeds are often sown during the first few minutes of a relationship.

When two cats meet for the first time, they stop and look at each other. If one hisses, the other bristles his coat and hisses back. However, if the first cat gives a little nudge with its cold nose, the other cat responds in kind, and they wind up purring together and licking each other's coats.

A man and a woman getting to know each other are like two little animals sniffing each other out. We do not have tails that wag or hair that bristles, but we do have eyes that narrow or widen. We have hands that flash knuckles or subconsciously soften in the palms-up 'I submit' position. There are dozens of other 'involuntary' reactions that take place in the first few moments of interaction. The good news is that we can learn to control these presumed involuntary reactions.

The moment you set eyes on each other, your Potential Love Partner subconsciously reads the subtleties of your body language. In these first crucial moments, he or she can unconsciously resolve to try for romantic take-off or abort thoughts of love. His or her mind then becomes computer-like, and your PLP continues to make rapid decisions about you during your *first* conversation, your *first* date.

In Part One, we will cover techniques to lure Potential Love Partners into approaching you, into liking you, and then into making a first date. I will share scientifically sound methods of keeping the conversation exciting and making the first date stimulating for your Quarry.

2 Similar Character, Complementary Needs

I Want a Lover Just Like Dear Old Me (Well, Almost)!

If you pass the first impressions test, you enter the second phase. Here your Quarry starts making judgments about you as a Potential Love Partner. His or her subconscious mind is saying, 'I want someone like me. Well, *almost* like me.'

If there is to be compatibility for a lifetime, or even for a date, some similarity is necessary. Our hearts are finely tuned instruments that seek someone who has values similar to ours, who holds beliefs similar to ours, and who looks at the world in more or less the same way we do. Similarity makes us feel good because it confirms the choices we have spent our whole lives making. We also look for people who enjoy the same activities so we can have fun together. Similarity is indeed a launch pad for a good relationship takeoff.

But we get bored with *too much* similarity. Besides, we need somebody to make up for our lacks. If we have no head for mathematics, who is going to balance the cheque book? If we are sloppy, who is going to pick up our socks?

So we also look for *complementary* qualities in a long-term love partner. But not *any* complementary qualities – only the ones we find interesting or that enhance our lives. Hence, we seek someone who is both *similar* and *complementary*.

In Part Two, we will explore methods of planting subliminal seeds of similarity in your Quarry's heart and ways to make him or her know that, even though you two are basically alike, you are different in so many utilitarian, fun, and interesting ways.

 ## 3 Equity

The 'WIIFM' Principle of Love

'Hey, sweetheart, everybody's got a market value! Everybody wears a price tag.' How pretty is she? How much prestige does he have? How blue is her blood? How much power does he wield? Are they rich, intelligent, nice? *What can they do for me?*

Does this sound ugly? Researchers tell us love is not really blind. Everybody – even the nicest people – has a touch of crass when it comes to choosing a long-term partner. It's no different to in the business world where everybody asks, 'WIIFM?' What's *in it for me?*

I can hear some of you protesting, 'No, love is pure and compassionate. It involves caring, altruism, communion, and selflessness. *That's* what love is all about.' Yes, that's what love *is* all about when good people are truly in love. You have probably even met couples who are deeply devoted and would sacrifice everything for each other. Yes, this kind of selfless love that we all dream of having exists. But it comes later – much later. It comes only *after* you have made your partner fall in love with you.

If you want to make someone fall in love with you, researchers say, you must initially convince them they are getting a good deal. We may not be conscious of it but, science tells us, tried and true market principles apply to love relationships. Lovers unconsciously calculate the other person's *comparable worth*, the *cost-benefit ratio* of the relationship, the *hidden costs*, the *maintenance fee*, and the *assumed depreciation*. Then they ask themselves, 'Is this the best offer I can get?' Everybody has a big scorecard locked away in their heart. And, in order to make people fall in love with you, you have to make them feel they are getting a very good deal.

Is all lost if you weren't born drop-dead gorgeous, or if you don't have a famous family name. No. In Part Three, we will explore silver-tongued verbal skills to replace the silver spoon that was never in our mouths when we were born. In that way, we can satisfy some very choosy Quarry.

 4 Ego

How Do You Love Me? Let Me Count the Ways

At the blazing core of first romantic rumblings is *ego*. Perhaps Cupid misses the mark when he aims his little arrow at Quarries' hearts. Science shows us where to really level our ammunition and take fire – right at their egos. People fall in love with people in whose eyes they behold the most ideal reflections of themselves.

Would-be lovers should be thrilled that ego makes the world go round, because Quarries' egos are very vulnerable targets. There are multifarious ways to make your Quarry feel beautiful, strong, handsome, charming, dynamic, or however he or she *wants* to feel. There are big-stroke compliments, little-stroke caresses, and a myriad of deliciously devious means to make your Quarry feel special. Subtle procedures can convince Quarries what they have suspected all along: 'I am different. I am wonderful. And to thank you for recognizing this amazing fact, I'll fall in love with you.'

Everyone also hungers for security and validation. We seek protection in our primary relationship from the cruel, cruel world. Part Four, *How to Make Anyone Fall in Love with You*, explores ways to make your Quarry feel that you are the salvation – you are his or her safe harbour from the storm of life.

 ## 5 Early-Date Gender-Menders

Is There Love After Eden?

Everyone smiled knowingly in 1956 when Rex Harrison moaned from the Broadway stage, 'Oh, why can't a woman be more like a man?' He knew his Fair Lady was a very different animal indeed. But in the era following *My Fair Lady*, feminists cast serious doubt on his convictions.

Now, after many decades of pondering, presuming, and postulating on whether men and women really differ in anything but their genitals, the envelope has been opened. The answer is – drumroll please – *yes*! Men and women think and communicate in dramatically different ways.

Neurosurgeons can point to clumps of neurons in female brains that cause men like Henry Higgins in *My Fair Lady* to call women 'exasperating, calculating, agitating, maddening, and infuriating'. Scientists aim their needles at the molecules in the male brain that make women accuse men of being 'insensitive clods'.

Despite the torrent of data flowing in about the genetic, cerebral, and sexual differences between men and women, both Hunters and Huntresses continue to *assume* we think alike and persist in courting each other in the way they would like to be courted themselves. Perhaps recent scientific findings will give men and women more insight into each other's style, but nothing short of a frontal lobotomy could make a permanent change in which brand of neurons our brains give off. Women will continue to be 'exasperating', and men will still be 'insensitive'. And both will keep on communicating in styles that turn each other off, especially on the first dates.

To avoid scaring off their prey before they bag it, serious big-game hunters know all the characteristics and habits of deer, moose, caribou, bison, and wild hogs. Likewise, serious love Hunters and Huntresses must be well versed in gender differences if they intend to make the kill.

Part Five briefs you on how to avoid the most common early-date turnoffs to make even the most wary Quarry comfortable letting down his or her guard. Love-shy Quarry who usually take flight when a man or woman gets too close will happily come within firing range of your arrow.

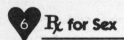

6 ℞ for Sex

How to Turn on the Sexual Electricity

Many books on how to turn on your partner make sex sound like flipping the switch on the night-light next to your bed. 'Press here to speed up orgasm. Stroke there for an extra charge.' Yes, sexuality *is* electricity, but your Quarry's bodily buttons only speed up or slow down the physical functions. *Mind power* is what drives the mighty machine and keeps it generating heat for many years. The most erotic organ in your Quarry's body is his or her *brain*.

For details and how-tos, there is no lack of reference books. They have names like *How to Drive Your Man Wild in Bed*, *How to Drive Your Woman Wild in Bed*, *How to Drive Your Man Even Wilder in Bed* and *How to Satisfy a Woman Every Time and Have Her Beg for More*. The list goes on. Such manuals are replete with detailed data for women on how to tickle that spot just below the 'cute little helmet' to drive him out of his gourd. Men can examine idiotproof charts on where to let their fingers do the walking so as to not miss the U-turn that leads to her G-spot.

All of this is important stuff – *very* important stuff. But when it comes to actually making somebody fall in love with you, it pales in comparison to what I will call *brain fellatio* – sucking the dreams, the longings, and the fantasies out of your Quarry, and then creating a lifelong erotic aura that he or she luxuriates in.

Gentlemen, far more important for a woman than how many times you can 'do it' in a week (or even in a night) is the sensuality and passion you create in every aspect of your relationship. And the *sensations* you give her every time you look at her. Ladies, far more important to a man than your bra-cup size or the curve of your hips, is the size and curve of your sexual *attitude* and how you deal with his individual sexuality.

No two sexualities are alike, just as no two snowflakes are alike. I will give you techniques to uncover your Quarry's unique sexuality and then make love to him or her just the way he or she likes it. In Part Six, we will explore the right kind of sex to make your particular Quarry fall in love with you.

Let us now embark upon our six-part journey, starting with what happens physically when we fall in love.

Chapter Three

The Physical Side of Falling in Love

 'Why Do My Insides Go All Funny?'

Falling in love is both a mental and a physical process. Some of the first techniques you will learn ignite your Quarry's physical response to you before his or her brain catches up. We will put love through the brain-scanner and under the x-ray machine to examine what physically happens to your Quarry when he or she starts to feel that incredible sensation called love.

 'Does Somebody Have to Be Pea-Brained to Fall in Love with Me?'

As a matter of fact, yes. Scientists tell us only PEA-brained people fall in love. At the core of infatuation, they speculate, is a chemical called phenylethylamine, or PEA. It is a chemical cousin of amphetamines and gives a similar 'kick'.

PEA comes from secretions through the nervous system and bloodstream that create an emotional response equivalent to a high on drugs. This is the chemical which makes your heart palpitate, your hands sweat, and your insides go all funny. (It is rumoured that PEA can also make you want to rip your Quarry's clothes off at the first available opportunity.)

Phenylethylamine, scientists say, along with dopamine and norepinephrine, is manufactured in the body when we first feel the physical sensation of romantic love. It is as close to a natural high as the body can get. (Cole Porter obviously knew what he was singing about when he wrote 'I get a kick out of you.')

The bad news is that the kick does not last forever, or even for very long. This adds to the quickly mounting scientific evidence that romantic love is relatively short-lived. That is why some people become 'love junkies'. The good news is that it *does* last long enough to kick-start great love affairs. Its average one-and-a-half to three-year duration is plenty of time to have a fantastic fling, to get him or her to say 'I do', and/or propagate the species.

Now, since you can't go around armed with a syringe filled with phenylethylamine, spot your Quarry, and inject the PEA-filled tube into his or her bloodstream, you do the next best thing. You develop techniques to trigger PEA-brained responses in people and give them the *sensation* that they are falling in love.

 ## 'Why Do We Fall in Love with One Person and Not Another?'

People don't just mysteriously wake up one morning with an overdose of PEA in their brains and then develop a crush on the next person they set eyes on. No, PEA and its sister chemicals are precipitated by emotional and visceral reactions to specific stimulus.

Like what? It can be a whiff of her perfume, the boyish way he says hello, or the adorable way she wrinkles her nose when she laughs. It could even be an innocuous article of clothing you are wearing that drives your Quarry bonkers. For example, in 1924, Conrad Hilton, the founder of the Hilton hotel chain, flipped over a red hat that he spotted sitting five pews in front of him in church. After the service, he followed the red hat down the street and eventually married the lady walking under it.

 ## 'How Can These Little Things Start Love?'

Why do these seemingly meaningless stimuli kick-start love? Where do they come from? Are they in our genes?

No, genes have nothing to do with falling in love. The origin lies deeply buried in our psyche. The ammunition that gets fired off when we see (hear, smell, feel) something we like is lying dormant in our subconscious. It springs from that apparently bottomless well from which most of our personality rises – our childhood experiences or, most significantly, what happens to us between the tender ages of five and eight. When we are very young, a type of subconscious *imprinting* takes place, similar to the phenomenon that occurs in certain species of the animal kingdom.

During the 1930s, an eminent Austrian ethologist, Dr Konrad Lorenz, induced a flock of baby ducks to become hopelessly attached to him. Observing how baby ducklings, shortly after hatching, begin to waddle along in single file behind their mother – and continue to do so into maturity – Dr Lorenz decided to imprint the ducklings with *himself*.

Lorenz hatched a clutch of duck eggs in an incubator. At first sight of their little beaks breaking through eggshells, he squatted low as if he were a mother duck and waddled past the eggs. They promptly broke free and followed him across the laboratory. Thereafter, despite the presence of real female ducks, these imprinted little ducklings continued to waddle after Dr Lorenz on every possible occasion.

Researchers have shown that the phenomenon of imprinting is not limited to birds. Various forms of it exist among fish, guinea pigs, sheep, deer, buffalo, and other mammalian species. Are humans immune to imprinting? Well, unlike the duped ducklings queued up behind Dr Lorenz, we do not continue to crawl after the doctor who delivered us until we reach adulthood. But there is strong evidence that we fall prey to another kind of imprinting – and early *sexual* imprinting.

Universally respected sexologist Dr John Money coined the term *Lovemap* to describe this imprinting. Our Lovemaps are carvings of pain or pleasure axed in our brains in early responses to our family members, our childhood friends, and our chance encounters. The cuts are so deep that they fester forever in some nook or cranny of the human psyche, just waiting to bleed again when the proper stimulus strikes.

Dr Money said, 'Lovemaps. They're as common as faces, bodies, and brains. Each of us has one. Without it there would be no falling in love, no mating, and no breeding of the species.'[7] Your Quarry has a Lovemap. You have a Lovemap. We all have Lovemaps. They are indelibly etched into our egos, our ids, our psyches, our subconscious. They can be positive imprintings. For example, perhaps your mother wore a certain perfume, your beloved father had a boyish grin, or your favourite teacher scrunched up her nose when she laughed. Perhaps a beautiful lady in a red hat was kind to little Connie Hilton when he was growing up in San Antonio, New Mexico.

Lovemaps can be negative, too. Women, maybe you were molested as a child, so now you can never love a man with a leering smile. Men, maybe your cruel wicked aunt wore Joy perfume, so now any woman who gives you a whiff of Joy makes you want to flee like a bug blasted with insect repellent.

Lovemaps sometimes contain very convoluted paths. Early negative experiences can give them a strange twist. Women, maybe your father ran off with another woman, leaving you and your mother alone, so now, if your date so much as glances at a passing lady, you freak out. Gentlemen, perhaps your beautiful baby-sitter spanked you when you were five, but it stimulated your little genitals and felt good. So now, as an adult, you cannot fall in love with a woman unless she will give you love spankings.

Forgotten experiences, both positive and negative, are remembered by your sexual subconscious. If the timing is right and someone triggers one, *BLAM!* A shot of PEA shoots through your veins. It blasts your brain, blinding you to reason, and you begin to fall in love. It's the necessary spark to kick-start love.

That is just for starters. The starter gets your car going, and then the battery takes over. Similarly, after your brain recuperates from its first shot of PEA, a little reason (hopefully) starts to make its way through the grey matter. As you and your PLP get to know each other better, you begin exploring your similarities and your differences (we cover this in Part Two), and you both start asking yourselves, 'What can I get from this relationship?' (Part Three). We listen to our ego and see how much reinforcement it is getting (Part Four). Early love is very delicate, and often we inadvertently turn our Quarry off in the first few dates (Part Five). If we get beyond that, what goes on – or doesn't go on – between the sheets plays a gigantic role (Part Six). Throughout *How to Make Anyone Fall in Love with You*, we will explore all these factors from a scientific point of view.

Let us now go back to the beginning. Where do you find a Potential Love Partner? How do you get that first shot of PEA shooting through his/her veins over you?

Chapter Four

Where Are All the Good Men and Women?

 ## Looking for Love in All the Wrong Places

Single and divorced people, young and old, all across America are asking themselves as they brush their teeth in the morning, as they shave or put on make-up, as they touch up the grey in their hair, 'Where are all the good men? Where are all the good women?'

'One in five Americans is single and searching,' *American Demographics* magazine tells us.[8] That means there are forty-nine million Americans aged twenty-five and older who are single, widowed, or divorced. And their number is growing.

'Good,' you say, 'but if there are so many Potential Love Partners around, where are they?' The answer is, 'They are everywhere – looking for love – just like you.' PLPs are sitting in the park munching a sandwich, enjoying music at a concert, walking the dog, riding the commuter train, and going to restaurants all around you.

Today, even with jet travel, on-line romances, and a shrinking globe, most people marry pretty close to home. Studies on what social scientists call *residential propinquity* show that Cupid's arrow does not travel far. In fact, one study tells us the median distance travelled by an unskilled worker to find his spouse is just five blocks.[9] Unless you have pitched your tent in the middle of the Sahara, you don't have to venture far for your hunting expedition. You will outfit yourself with some new knowledge and, armed with the techniques in this book, you can start tracking Quarry very close at hand.

You have heard the wail of unsuccessful lovers: 'I'm looking for love in all the wrong places, looking for love in all the wrong faces.' That is not the real problem. Most have been looking for love in all the wrong *ways.*

Theatrical performers know they need a different set of skills to get cast from an audition than they need to sustain a role on stage. They must immediately knock producers out with their talent, sometimes in one minute or less. Likewise, you need different skills to make someone fall in love with you than you need to keep a relationship warm for a lifetime. You must knock your Quarry out – sometimes in the first minute or less. Without that strong first kick, he or she might never get to know you, let alone fall in love with you.

Chapter Five

Does Love at First Sight Exist?

Let's say you get lucky tomorrow and spot a Potential Love Partner. He or she is sitting on the steps reading a book. Or standing in a museum studying a painting. Or getting on the bus. Or waiting in line at the bank cash machine.

You sneak a second peek. Something about the stranger revs up your internal PEA factory, and a little dollop goes squirting through your veins. Maybe it's her looks, the way he moves, something she is wearing. Her aura? Is this love at first sight? Does love at first sight even exist?

Well, that is a semantics question. Instant desire, or lust at first sight, definitely exists. However, the scientific world pretty well agrees that love at first sight is merely wisdom after the event.

'A successful love affair, perhaps one leading to marriage, is retrospectively declared to be true love; whereas if one is rebuffed, it is classified ... as infatuation'

Medical Aspects of Human Sexuality[10]

Semantics aside, one fact remains. any small stimulus can kick-start love. Your first moves when you spot a Potential Love Partner are crucial. If, from that powerful stimulus, love grows, you have every right to call it love at first sight. Nobody will argue with you.

Love at first sight has survived because it is an integral part of the many popular beliefs about romantic love. In the same way that a voodoo curse causes death only in persons who believe in its power to kill them, love at first sight truly exists for those who believe in it.

Part One

First Impressions

*You Never Get a Second Chance
at Love at First Sight*

Chapter Six

How to Make a Dynamite First Impression

 First Impressions Last Forever

The first moment your Quarry lays eyes on you has awesome potency. The picture burns its way into his or her eyes and can stay emblazoned in your Quarry's memory forever.

I have a dear friend, an older gentleman named Gerald, who is very sought after in the social scene of his home town. He is a charming escort for several elderly ladies who long ago lost their husbands. Gerald met these women when they were all in high school together back in the late 1940s. His women friends are inwardly beautiful; however, physically, several have gained weight and have long since lost their youthful attractiveness.

Once, at a party, I overheard a rude man tease Gerald about his taste in women. My friend was genuinely confused at the tactless remark.

'But they are all *beautiful*!' Gerald exclaimed. He reached into his wallet and pulled out an old, dog-eared black-and-white photograph of his high school homecoming queen and her court.

'See?' Gerald said to the man. Two of the three ladies he was currently escorting were in the photo. One of them was the homecoming queen. To this day, Gerald sees his lady friends as beautiful as they were back in 1948. Such is the power of first impressions.

Image consultants are paid thousands of dollars to pontificate in boardrooms across America, 'You never get a second chance to make a first impression.' The adage has been given the exalted status of a proverb: 'First impressions are most lasting.' So what else is new?

What is new is this: Even as we enter the 21st century, we do not really comprehend the unbelievable compass and consequence of first impressions. Or on what lilliputian details they are sometimes based.

Gentlemen, one backward baseball cap or gold chain flashing through the hair on your chest can make or break a budding relationship with the lady before you even say 'hi'. Ladies, one quarter of a turn away when he ventures 'hello' can turn the handsome prince back into a frightened frog.

Be Ready for Love – Always!

If first impressions are so crucial and a Potential Love Partner makes the 'go/no go' decision within seconds of spotting you, here is the big question: why do people looking for love spend so much time making themselves attractive when they go out on a date but so little when they take the dog to the vet? By the time you have the date, your Quarry's first impression of you has already been set. How you look on the date is, of course, important. But it is not nearly as decisive as his or her first glimpse of you.

You don't realize it, but here is the sad truth: you have probably let dozens of PLPs get away in recent months just because your trap was not set – you were not fixed up for the kill. Hunters, that means you were not dressed for the part.

Huntresses, that means you were not groomed properly. Research shows that for men, clothes are more crucial to first impressions. For women, it is her body and face.

Huntresses, you may well ask, 'Is make-up all that important?' Let's go to the studies. Researchers asked men to talk with six different women who sometimes wore make-up, sometimes didn't. Their study, 'Lipstick as a Determiner of First Impressions of Personality', revealed that the male opinion of each woman was *very different* when she wore lipstick.[11]

Women, how many times, sauntering down the street without your make-up, have you spotted Handsome Stranger, who does not even look your way? If he is a typical male attracted by rosy lips and nice big eyes, what do you expect? Men, how many times, in your grungy clothes, have you tried to talk to Lovely Lady on the bus who gives you a cursory answer and looks away? If she is a typical woman attracted by an air of competence and success, what do you expect?

TECHNIQUE 1

Dress for 'The Kill' – Everywhere

Men, this does *not* mean you have to don your three-piece suit to buy the newspaper. Women, it does *not* mean you need to slap on three coats of mascara to walk the dog. What it does mean is whenever you step out the door, step out dressed to kill ... your Quarry.

We get lazy about first impressions due to the reinforcement theory. Say you fix yourself up for the kill. You go out to walk the dog three times, four times, looking like a traffic stopper, and nothing happens.

So you say, 'This doesn't work.'

In my sales seminars, I tell participants that the average sale is not made until after the fifth sales call. Give it some time. Can't you wait five more dog-walks for your future beloved to say, 'Nice doggy. What's his name? And, by the way, what's yours?'

 ## Stay Psychologically 'Fit to Kill'

Not only should you be physically ready, you must keep your *mental* doors open to let love walk in ... wherever you are. PLPs do not just enter your life from parties and singles' clubs.

Cindy is an attractive young manicurist who has been doing my nails for several years. (There must be some drug in nail polish remover that dissolves women's inhibitions and induces them to spill every detail of their lives as they hold hands across the manicure table). For months Cindy has been griping to me that, in her line of work, she only meets women.

I had a late appointment with Cindy one evening at about six o'clock. She was telling me how, after a long day of clipping, filing, and painting, she is too tired to go out to singles' bars to try to meet someone. At about 6:45 p.m., the door opened behind Cindy's back. We heard a deep male voice say, 'Excuse me, I know it's terribly late. But is it possible to get a manicure?' I looked up over Cindy's shoulder and beheld a Greek god. (I had no idea such deities needed manicures!) Before I could pull my jaw back up, Cindy, not even turning around, said, 'Nope, we close in ten minutes.'

'How do ya like that?' she grumbled, keeping her gaze fixed on my hangnail as he walked out. 'Who does he think he is to march in here at this hour and expect a manicure?'

Then, Cindy's ears, finely tuned to such trappings as expensive sports cars, heard a Jaguar revving up outside her window. She jumped up to look, and there was her Adonis careening out of the car park, and out of her life, forever in his sleek chariot. She didn't stop kicking herself long enough for me to respectfully suggest that one should keep one's eyes open all the time for such opportunities.

Top producers in the sales profession never stop prospecting – in the dentist's office, in the copy shop, at the pizzeria. One salesman friend of mine clinched a multimillion-dollar corporate insurance deal with another nude man he met in his health club Jacuzzi. You can, as the old song says, 'find a million-dollar baby in a five-and-ten-cent store'.

TECHNIQUE 2

Stay Psychologically 'Fit to Kill'

Big-game hunters lay bear traps even before they spot the bear. Fishermen cast nets long before the shoal swims their way. If you set your psychological trap the minute your feet hit the floor in the morning, chances are the next big one won't get away.

Now you are physically and mentally ready for love. The next question is, 'How can I make my Quarry's *insides go all funny* when he or she meets me?'

Let's start with two of the most potent weapons you need to trigger love at first sight. They are right above your nose. Many people swear, 'I fell in love the moment I looked into my lover's eyes.'

Chapter Seven

How to Ignite Love at First Sight

A man may be classified as a breast man, a buttocks man, or a leg man. And, although many women will insist otherwise, most women are certified butt watchers. (This is not just idle conjecture: a British study determined that these are people's favourite eyeball destinations.)[12]

But researchers have ascertained that *everybody* is an eye person. When you were a teenager being reluctantly or otherwise introduced to strangers, your parents probably told you, 'Look straight into their eyes.' And then they would tell you in no uncertain terms that any of the aforementioned anatomical locations were strictly off limits.

Powerful eye contact immediately stimulates strong feelings of affection. This was proved once and for all in a study called 'The Effects of Mutual Gaze on feelings of Romantic Love.'[13] Researchers put forty-eight men and women who didn't know each other in a big room. They gave them directions on how much eye contact to have with their partners during casual conversation. Afterward, the researchers asked each participant how he or she felt about the various people they had spoken with.

The results?

Subjects who were gazing at their partner's eyes and whose partner was gazing back reported significantly higher feelings of affection than subjects in any other condition . . . Subjects who engaged in mutual gaze increased significantly their feelings of passionate love ... and liking for their partner.

Journal of Research in Personality [14]

Let's say that in less technical language: locking eyeball to eyeball with the attractive stranger helps put the match to the flame of love.

Why does eye contact have such fiery consequences? Anthropologist Helen Fisher says it is basic animal instinct. Direct eye contact triggers 'a primitive part of the human brain, calling forth one of two basic emotions – approach or retreat.' [15]

Unrelenting eye contact creates a highly emotional state similar to fear. When you look directly and potently into someone's eyes, his or her body produces chemicals like phenylethylamine, or PEA, that jolts the *sensation* of being in love. Thus, making strong, almost threatening intense eye contact with your Quarry is one of the first steps in making him or her fall in love with you.

People look lingeringly at sights they like and quickly avert their eyes from those they don't. We enjoy gazing for long, lazy hours into a cosy fire, yet our hands jerk up to shield our eyes from an atrocious movie scene. It's the same when looking at people. We gaze lovingly at our lovers, yet avert our eyes from unpleasant, ugly, or dull people. When someone bores us, the first part of our body to escape is our eyes.

I am acutely aware of this phenomenon during my speeches. Whenever I drone on too long about a particular point, audience members bury their noses in their notes. Inspecting their manicures takes on prime importance. Some even nod off.

When I get back on track, their eyes flutter up like butterflies returning to the sunshine after a rainstorm.

Another, almost opposite, factor that blocks good eye contact is shyness. The more someone overwhelms us, the more we avoid his or her eyes. Very low-ranking employees often avert their gaze from the big boss. If we meet someone extraordinarily handsome, beautiful, or accomplished, we tend to do the same.

In my seminars, I strive to make eye contact with everyone in the audience. However, if there is an especially handsome man in the sea of faces, I often find myself avoiding his gaze. I look into the eyes of everybody *but* him. Then, realizing the folly of my ways, I force myself to look into the eyes of Very Attractive Male, and *BLAM*! My heart skips a beat. I sometimes lose my train of thought, I stutter.

Powerful stuff, this eye contact.

How Much Eye Contact Does it Take to Imitate Love?

A British scientist determined that, on average, when talking, people look at one another only 30 to 60 per cent of the time. This is not enough to rev up the engines of love at first sight.

While he was still a graduate student at the University of Michigan, a prominent psychologist named Zick Rubin became fascinated with how to measure love. Later, at Harvard and Brandeis, the romantic young researcher produced the first psychometrically based scale to determine how much affection couples felt for each other. It became known as *Rubin's Scale* and, to this day, many social psychologists use it to determine people's feelings for each other.

In his study on the 'Measurement of Romantic Love', Zick Rubin found that people who were deeply in love gaze at each other much more when talking and are slower to look away when somebody intrudes in their world.[16] He confirmed this through a trick experiment. He asked dating couples a long series of questions so he could first rate the pairs on how much they loved each other. The couples, unaware of their rating, were then put in a waiting room and told, 'The experimenter will be with you shortly to start the experiment.' Unbeknownst to them, that *was* the experiment. Hidden cameras recorded how much time the couples spent staring into each other's eyes. The higher the couple had scored on the first test, the more time they spent looking at each other. The less love they felt for each other, the less time they made eye contact.

To give your Quarry the subliminal sense that the two of you are *already* in love (a self-fulfilling prophecy), dramatically increase your eye contact while the two of you are chatting. Push it up to 75 per cent of the time or more if you want to get the PEA gushing through his or her veins.

The extra seconds of eye contact speak silent volumes. To a woman, the volumes will read, 'Beautiful lady, I am intrigued by you. I am fascinated by what you are saying.' A man might interpret the increased eye contact as, 'I'm ravenous for you. I can't wait to tear your clothes off and have you make mad passionate love to me.'

You *must*, however, look right into your Quarry's eyes if you want to excite those feelings of love at first sight. Not at his eyebrows, not at the bridge of her nose – look right into those baby blues, browns, grays, or greens. Pretend you are admiring the optic nerve behind the eyeballs.

Wisdom for the ages gleaned from *The King and I* is 'Whistle a happy tune, and you will be happy.' Likewise, give off signals of the two of you being in love, and your Quarry will feel sensations of love.

TECHNIQUE 3

Intense Gaze

When conversing with your Quarry, exaggerate your eye contact. Search for his or her optic nerve. Lock eyes with your Quarry to give the aura of *already* being in love.

There is more to it than just looking deeply into someone's eyes, however. You must make your own eyes warm and inviting. Staring into the frigid eyes of a dead fish does nothing to incite love.

How to Get Sexy 'Bedroom Eyes'

Bedroom eyes is not just a quality movie stars are blessed with. Neither Bette Davis nor Clark Gable had a patent on them. We all have that suggestive look buried deep in our evolutionary psyche. Ethnologists have even named it the *copulatory gaze*. The copulatory gaze plays a big role in lovemaking. For example, before having sex, pygmy chimpanzees – which are about as close to human as an ape can get – spend several moments staring deeply into each other's eyes.

Sex *without* eye contact is difficult for some primates. Several Finnish researchers introduced male and female baboons to each other. With blinder devices, they varied what part of the female's anatomy the male baboon got a gander at first. When the male's initial glimpse of his lady love was her genitals, only five ejaculations occurred. However, when he first gazed into her eyes *before* getting a peek at her privates, twenty-one ejaculations occurred.[17] (Men, increasing eye contact during foreplay does not promise you twenty-one ejaculations, but it definitely encourages affectionate feelings from your female.)

Anthropologist Helen Fisher goes so far as to say, 'Perhaps it is the eye – not the heart, the genitals, or the brain – that is the initial organ of romance.'[18]

What makes your eyes sexy and inviting? Quite simply, *large pupils*. Incidentally, examine old photographs of Bette Davis or Clark Gable, and you will see enormously expanded pupils. Undoubtedly a retouching job, but, hey!

The father of a science which became known as *pupillometrics*, Dr Eckhard Hess, demonstrated that large pupils were more alluring by showing two pictures of a woman's face to a group of men. The pictures were identical except, in one of them, Hess had retouched the lady's pupils to make them larger. The male response to Ms Big Pupils was twice as strong as to the identical woman with small pupils. Hess then reversed the experiment and showed pictures of men with enlarged pupils to women. There was the same positive female response to Mr Big Pupils.

Dr Hess tells us that we cannot *consciously* control our pupil size, but in the early 1960s he proved that we can at least manipulate it. He hooked male subjects up to a Rube Goldberg device to measure their pupil fluctuations and proceeded to show them a series of photographs. When the men saw pictures of a landscape, a baby, or a family, their pupils fluctuated a little. However, Hess sneaked a picture of a naked woman into the pile. When the men got an eyeful of that one, zing went the strings of their pupils, thus proving that when we look at an enticing stimulus, our pupils expand.

Here is how to enlarge your pupils to make your eyes look like inviting pools your Quarry will willingly drown in. While the two of you are chatting, simply gaze at the most attractive feature on your Quarry's face. Does she have a cute little nose? Does he have an adorable dimple? As your eyes enjoy the sight, your pupils gradually enlarge. Keep your eyes off that mole with the black hair growing out of it. That will make your pupils slap shut like snapdragons!

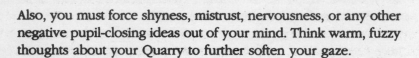

TECHNIQUE 4

Bedroom Eyes

While chatting with your Quarry, gaze at the most attractive part of his or her face. Your pupils will automatically expand, giving you those bedroom eyes.

Also, think loving thoughts. Concentrate on how beautiful your Quarry is, how comfortable you feel with her, how much fun it would be to take a shower with him.

Also, you must force shyness, mistrust, nervousness, or any other negative pupil-closing ideas out of your mind. Think warm, fuzzy thoughts about your Quarry to further soften your gaze.

How to Awaken Primal, Unsettling, Sexy Feelings in Your Quarry

Let us now talk about a third technique with your initial organ of romance. This one gives your Quarry that primal, unsettling feeling that floods over people when they start to fall in love.

When conversing, people tend to look briefly away at the end of a sentence or during silences, *except* when they are engrossed in the listener (or hopelessly in love). The phrase, *he couldn't take his eyes off her* is not just allegoric. People who love each other not only indulge in much more eye contact while talking, but they are more hesitant to take their eyes off each other, even *after* they finish speaking. It is electrifying when someone's glance lingers on you during the silence, after you have stopped talking.

Several years ago, I hired a carpenter to put an additional window in my office. Jerry was not terribly good-looking, and he certainly was no mental colossus, but for some inexplicable reason, I found him very attractive. There was an indefinable, mysterious quality about Jerry. It was unsettling, primal, sexy.

I did not permit myself to indulge in my little infatuation, however. Perhaps I thought seducing the carpenter was neither politically correct nor otherwise desirable under the circumstances. Or perhaps Jerry's other qualities weren't emblazoned on my Lovemap. However, thoughts of Jerry filled my fantasies for weeks.

I didn't see him for several years. Then, just recently, while working on this book, I needed shelves to hold my research materials. Naturally, I called Jerry. He arrived on my doorstep, ten pounds heavier, three years older, but just as sexy. This time, thanks to my recent research, five minutes into our conversation, I realized why he turned me on.

Every time I said something Jerry's eyes lingered on mine. After I had finished speaking, even during the silences, his eyes stayed glued to mine. That quality, I realized, is what I had found so unsettling, so primal, so *sexy*.

As our discussion about my shelves progressed, I also realized *why* Jerry was holding the eye contact longer. He wasn't trying to be sexy. He wasn't fascinated by me. It wasn't because he couldn't take his eyes off me. It was simply because Jerry wasn't too bright, and it took an extra beat for my 'I'd like the shelves eleven inches wide' to sink into his brain.

We now turn this into a technique to awaken those primal, unsettling, sexy feelings and give your new PLP a jolt.

TECHNIQUE 5

Sticky Eyes

Whenever you are talking with your Quarry, let your eyes stay glued to his or hers a little longer – even during the silences.

A gaze that stays overtime awakens primal, slightly disturbing feelings. It induces the same 'fight or flight' chemicals that race through our veins when we feel infatuation.

When we must look away, do so reluctantly. Drag your eyes away slowly, as though they had been stuck with warm toffee.

Naughty Eyes Are So Nice

Now we come to the last way our eyes can get the chemicals flowing through our Quarry's veins. There are carefully choreographed steps that a man and a woman must take upon meeting each other if love is going to develop.

One of those can't-do-without steps involves our eyes. A curious phenomenon happens to the eyes when a man and a woman begin to feel comfortable with each other and the rumblings of love start to resonate through their bodies. As lovers are lulled by the good feelings, their eyes become more courageous. They slowly start to wander lovingly over each other's faces, hair, eyes. Then they become bolder and venture down to their partner's shoulders, neck, and torso. A dreaminess sets in.

To push your relationship with a new Quarry into this next step of intimacy, use the technique I call *visual voyage*. As the conversation progresses, let your eyes slide down from the nose to the lips. Caress the lips with your eyes for a moment or two, then slowly venture south to the neck and, if all is going well, beyond.

TECHNIQUE 6

A Visual Voyage

As you and your Quarry are chatting, let your eyes do some travelling – but only on safe territory at first. Take a visual voyage all over his or her face, concentrating mostly on the eyes. If he or she seems to be enjoying your expedition, take small side trips to the neck, shoulders, and torso.

Women, you have a more liberal passport to travel in this territory. Men, be more wary. You are cruising into dangerous seas and can sink the ship if your eyes travel too far south and vacation there too long.

These four eye techniques – *intense gaze, bedroom eyes, sticky eyes*, and *visual voyage* – are scientifically proven aphrodisiacs. When you start using them on your Quarry, you will feel the effect. However, you don't need science to tell you that you cannot make someone fall in love with you unless the two of your are introduced to each other. Unless, of course, you engineer an acquaintance without the benefit of introduction. In the vernacular, that's 'pick them up'. Proponents of political correctness would recoil at the term. But I, for one, have nothing against the concept – if the 'pickup' is done in a manner, shall we say, befitting the situation and the individuals involved.

Let us now cover some basics. We will explore how you can engineer the acquaintance of a Potential Love Partner without the benefit of third-party introduction.

Chapter Eight
Your First Approach

The Gentle Art of Pickup (Not for Men Only)

Biologists, as they watch animals spotting each other, sniffing, growling, hissing, nuzzling, and finally copulating, observe the same courtship rituals over and over. The identical patterns of proceptivity and aggression repeat themselves time and time again. If the pattern is broken, often copulation does not take place.

It is no different with Homo sapiens (that's us), but we operate with a serious handicap. Unlike those of lover animals, our brains get in the way of our instincts. In other words, we think too much. We ask ourselves, and others around us, too many questions. 'Will he think I'm forward? Should I play hard to get? Do I look alright? Is my tie straight? Maybe I should go to the ladies' room and put on some more lipstick first.' Shyness often takes over and paralyses us, like a deer frozen in car headlights.

Rabbits have no such reflections. Nor should *we*, when we spot our Quarry. We must merely follow what research tells us are the right moves when we spot him or her.

Hunters, Make the First Move ... *Fast*

Gentlemen, what are the right moves when you spot a woman you think you would like to make part of your future? No argument here. You must approach, and you must do it fast. The old chestnut 'he who hesitates is lost' is a rock-hard nut in the singles' jungle.

Once a male friend (a PMF, or platonic male friend, as we called non-romantic male friends in secondary school) and I were dining at a restaurant. My PMF, Phil, spotted a strikingly beautiful woman sitting alone at the bar behind him. He turned back to me and announced, 'That's the woman I'm going to marry!'

'Congratulations. So how do you intend to go about meeting her?' I challenged.

'Let's see,' he mused. 'Perhaps I'll just go up to her and say hello. No,' he decided. 'That's too mundane for my future bride. Maybe I'll go and offer to buy her a drink. No, that's too trite. Possibly,' he joked. 'I'll go tell her I'm passionately in love with her. No, that's too forward. Shall I tell her I want to make her the mother of my children? No, that's premature.'

While Phil was bantering on about his approach, I watched over his shoulder as a good-looking man marched right up to Phil's intended and sat on the empty stool next to her. By the time my friend turned around, the newcomer and Phil's never-to-be bride were in deep conversation. 'Love at first sight' became Phil's 'loss at first sight'. As it usually does for a Hunter who hesitates.

When you spot an attractive lady, what is the best strategy? Let your body do the talking. First, use your eyes. Look at her and hold your eye contact for a few extra seconds. Be prepared for her to look away. A woman has been trained to lower her eyes when a man looks at her. *This does not mean she is not interested.* An analysis of flirtation patterns tells us if, after looking away, the woman looks up again within 45 seconds, she welcomes your attention.

Gentlemen, set your chronograph. As she coyly feigns interest in something else in the room, clock how long it takes for her to glance back at you. If it's within 45 seconds, proceed as follows.

Smile at her and give her a little nod. Think of it as making a reservation for a table at an exclusive restaurant. When you have signalled a woman's attention, you have made your reservation to talk to her. Abolish all thoughts of 'What will she think of me if I'm too forward or move too fast?' She won't think *anything* of you – good or bad – if you don't meet her. If you don't *move fast, every* woman will be the one that got away.

TECHNIQUE 7 (FOR HUNTERS):

Move Fast

'Move fast' doesn't mean making a beeline for your Quarry and jumping her bones. It simply means immediately making your presence known by signalling your interest. Here is the best proven method.

Make eye contact. Maintain steady eye contact with her and hold it just a tad too long.

Smile at her. Make sure your smile is friendly and respectful, not a leering grin or a salacious smirk.

Give her a nod. If she returns your gaze within the decisive 45 seconds, nod slightly. The nod reads, 'I like you. May I make a reservation to talk with you?'

Move within her range. The final step is to move close enough to her to talk.

You are now in position for conversation. What should you say to her first? Abolish the words *opening line* from your thoughts. Generic lines come across just like that – lines. After my love seminars, many a shy Hunter has asked me, 'What's a good opening line?' I find it charming that men ponder such dilemmas.

Once an extremely shy chap attending my seminar pulled a dog-eared book out of his pocket called *How to Pick up Girls*. Apparently he was not the first to seek such guidance. The book is twenty-five years old and has sold over two million copies, primarily through advertising in men's magazines. It suggests antique gems like, 'Don't tell me a beautiful girl like you doesn't have a date tonight' and 'Are you a model?' This scintillating repartee may have worked when Dad met Mum, but in our more enlightened times, women abhor lines. Far more significant that what you say is how you look and how you say *whatever* you say.

Gentlemen, your opening words should relate to the woman or the current situation. Ask her what time it is. Compliment her watch or her outfit. Ask her for directions. Inquire how she knows the host or hostess of the party. In fact, the less clever your opener, the better, because this early in your relationship, she is not metabolizing your words – she is checking you out. Her brain is hard at work sizing you up on your manner and your words. Whatever you say, she *knows* it is just an excuse for you to talk to her. If she likes you, that is fine with her.

Although you should not memorize any line, *do* pay attention to the first words which flow from your lips. Just as the first glimpse of you should please your Quarry's eyes, so should your first words delight her ears. Remember, that first sentence to your Quarry is 100 per cent of her sampling of you so far. If you open with a complaint, in her book you will be a complainer. If you open with a conceited remark, she will label you a braggart. But if your first words charm her, she will find you charming.

Gentlemen, you may be wondering why you have to play it cool. Why do you have to be so subtle, controlled, and precise in your approach? It all goes back to nature. Buried deep in a woman's instincts, when she looks at you, is a subconscious judgment of you as a possible partner. She wants to feel you are captivated by her. But she also wants to know that you can control your animal passion, thus demonstrating what a suave and effective partner you would be in life.

Huntresses, Make the Fast Move ... *First*

Huntresses, you may think the responsibility for the pickup rests on the man's shoulders. Surprisingly enough, though, research shows that women initiate two-thirds of all encounters.

This, too, is part of nature's grand design. In the animal kingdom, wannabe-lovers attract each other by hooting, crowing, or stomping the ground. They are more overt than Homo sapiens are. A female chimpanzee in heat will spot her Quarry, 'stroll up to the male, and tip her buttocks towards his nose to get his attention. Then she'll actually pull him up to his feet to copulate.'[19] This behaviour is known as *female proceptivity*. Female proceptivity (as opposed to *receptivity*) is not unknown to our species, although we are, I should hope, a little less obvious.

How do women initiate encounters? The same way kids do. The same way the birds, the bees, and all the wonderful animals in God's kingdom do: with an attention-getting device.

Ladies, let's say you behold Mr Handsome Stranger dancing at the disco, seated across the table from you, or huffing and puffing on the next StairMaster at the gym. What should you do? The usual scenario goes something like this. Upon spotting him, a woman locks eyes with him for a split second and then glances away. More courageous women flash a little smile and *then* look away, hoping that he will then take the initiative (after all, she doesn't want to appear forward.).

As fifty thousand tiny seeds blow from a flower and only one takes root, your chances at love might as well be one in fifty thousand with Mr Handsome Stranger if this is your entire attack. You must do more than just flash a little smile and leave the rest to nature.

First Moves That Work for Women

Let's look at the studies and see what *works*. A researcher named Monica Moore heard that women made two-thirds of the approaches and wanted to find out exactly how they did so. She set up a study where she observed more than two hundred women at a party and recorded what are scientifically known as their *non-verbal solicitation signals*.

Here, in descending order, are the results of Monica Moore's findings. The number following each move is the number of times Moore saw it work successfully during the experiment.[20] Need I spell it out? Huntresses, these are the moves that make a man come over and talk to you at a party.

How Women Successfully Make the First Move

Smile at him broadly	511
Throw him a short, darting glance	253
Dance alone to the music	253
Look straight at him and flip your hair	139
Keep a fixed gaze on him	117
Look at him, toss your head, then look back	102
'Accidentally' brush up against him	96
Nod your head at him	66
Point to a chair and invite him to sit	62
Tilt your head and touch your exposed neck	58
Lick your lips during eye contact	48
Primp while keeping eye contact with him	46
Parade close to him with exaggerated hip movement	41
Ask for his help with something	34
Tap something to get his attention	8
Pat his buttocks (My note: not advised!)	8

Sisters, do *not* be hesitant about making the first move. If you need more courage, think of it this way. Female choice is an evolutionary mandate given to a woman so she may select the best mate and thus assure the survival of the species. You are merely fulfilling your instinctive destiny when you overtly lure Mr Handsome Stranger. Mother Nature would approve.

Still shy? Do you feel he will think you are too forward if you smile broadly at him in the crowd or 'accidentally' brush up against him? He won't, because, happily, the male ego takes over ... retroactively. Ten minutes later, he won't even realize that he was not the one who made the initial overture. Researcher Moore said that men think they are making the first move when they are actually responding to women's non verbal overtures.

I decided to add my own research to Monica Moore's established findings when I was dining alone recently at one of the ubiquitous TGIF restaurants in Albany, New York. I was giving a talk the following morning to a singles' group, so as I was finishing dinner, I was running the next day's seminar programme over in my mind. In my talk, I planned a segment on the 'smile', in which I would tell women how important it is to smile at an attractive man.

I thought to myself, 'Leil, you hypocrite. Tomorrow morning you'll be telling women to have the courage to smile at strangers, and you don't even have the nerve to do it yourself.' While ruminating over this, I spotted a good-looking man reading while finishing his dinner a few tables from me. I thought, 'OK, Leil, courage. Let's try it.' So I smiled at this handsome stranger.

The poor chap looked a little stunned and dove his astonished nose back into his book. Soon after, he looked up again. I smiled again. Once more his nose disappeared in his reading material. A few minutes later, the handsome stranger got up and walked past my table to go to the men's room. As he passed, I forced myself to smile yet again. The perplexed fellow kept on walking, scratching his head.

Then things got interesting. On the way back from the men's room, he walked very slowly by my table. Once more I looked up at him and – you guessed it – smiled. Mr Handsome Stranger stopped walking. After the flood of smiles I had drowned him in, it was perfectly logical to start chatting as if we had been formally introduced. He joined me at my table for coffee.

Well, I invited this gentleman – his name was Sam – to attend my seminar the next morning, which he did. To illustrate the 'smile' part of my seminar, I told the audience the story (without revealing Sam's identity, of course) of how my smile had engineered a meeting with the lone diner.

After the seminar, Sam said, 'You know, Leil, I suppose you were talking about me in that little story you told. But,' he added, looking thoroughly confused and quite sincere, 'I thought it was *I* who made the approach to *you*.' Of course, Sam.

I tell you, Sisters, the male ego is a wondrous thing. Have the courage to smile broadly, nod, point to a chair, and invite him to sit – or choose almost any of Monica Moore's manoeuvres – and he will forget that he didn't make the first approach.

TECHNIQUE 8 (FOR HUNTRESSES):

Move First

Huntresses, when you spot a possible Quarry, do not wait for his approach. Nature decrees that *you* must make the first move. Use any of the proven ploys. It is as close to jabbing his buttocks with a syringe filled with PEA as you can get.

Chapter Nine
Your First Body Language

Let Your Body Do the Talking

Science documents that early body language of both partners is crucial to whether love will develop or not. One of the most tireless researchers in the laboratory of love was Dr Timothy Perper, who spent more than two thousand gruelling hours perched on stools of singles' bars, scrutinizing men, women, and their early courting moves.

Like researchers tracking the mating habits of hamsters, Dr Perper spotted the identical courtship pattern repeatedly in his singles' bar laboratory. Night after night, he stayed resolutely at his post, scribbling notations, devising charts, and hypothesizing formulae as men and women picked each other up. Then, in the finest scientific tradition, he broke the body language pattern of couples getting to know each other into five very specific steps.

Dr Perper's findings reveal that when both partners stuck to a precise sequence of moves, the couple wound up leaving together or making a date. However, if either partner broke the sequence – even accidentally – the couple drifted apart.

Many people looking for love take lessons in social dancing hoping to meet a Potential Lover Partner. They painstakingly learn the steps to the fox trot, the waltz, the cha-cha, and the rhumba. But they fall flat on their faces in the most important dance of all, the one the good doctor dubbed *the Dance of Intimacy*.

What are the steps to the Dance of Intimacy? They are as clear and as carefully choreographed as those of the Tennessee Waltz. They are the sequential movements you *must* make if intimacy is to develop with your PLP. Pay attention to each of the following five subconscious body language steps because, if you slip on any of them, your Quarry will lose interest and wander back into the singles' jungle.

The Dance of Intimacy

Step One: Non-verbal Signal After the two partners are within speaking range, one or the other makes his or her presence known (as described in the previous chapter) by a smile, a nod, or a glance.

Step Two: Talk One of the two then speaks. Perhaps he or she makes a comment or asks a question. Even a simple 'Hi' will do, but something verbal takes place.

Step Three: Turning Now it gets interesting. When one partner throws out the verbal signal, the recipient *must* turn at least the head fully toward the speaker and acknowledge the comment receptively. If he or she does not, the Hunter seldom tries again.

However, if the partner *does* turn warmly toward the speaker, they fall into conversation. Then a crucial pivoting takes place. Hunter and Quarry gradually switch from just their heads turned toward each other to their shoulders. If they like each other, their torsos soon turn, followed by their knees. Finally, in successful meetings, their whole bodies wind up facing each other.

This head-to-head, belly-to-belly, knees-to-knees gradual sequence can take from minutes to hours. With each increasing turn, intimacy increases. With each turn away, intimacy decreases.

Step Four: Touching Concomitant with talking and gradually turning toward each other comes a powerful aphrodisiac, touch. A slight brush of his hand while he passes you a pretzel. A light touch on your jacket as she whisks away a piece of thread. The touch is fleeting, almost imperceptible.

How you respond to his or her first touch is a big factor in whether the interaction continues or not. If he or she brushes your jacket and you slightly stiffen your shoulders, your partner can subliminally interpret this as rejection – often wrongly. But it is too late.

At this point in the progression, Dr Perper tells us, it becomes impossible to tell which is Hunter and which is Quarry. Once the initial touch has been executed, well received, and even returned, the man and woman are on their way to becoming, at least for the duration of the evening, a couple.

At about this point, yet another phenomenon takes place. Eye contact takes on a different character. As early as 1977, a researcher observed escalating eye contact in couples as they went from more formal eye contact to gazing. Their eyes gradually embarked on travels all over each other's faces, hair, necks, shoulders, and torsos.[21] This is the *visual voyage* we talked about earlier.

Step Five: Synchronization The final step is the most fascinating to watch. As though to confirm their newfound affection for each other, the couple begins to move in synchronicity with each other.

For example, the man and woman may reach for their drinks at the same time and put their glasses back on the table together. Then they progress to subconsciously shifting weight together, swaying to the music together, turning their heads to some outside interruption together, and then simultaneously looking back at each other.

Dr Perper wrote, 'Once synchronized, couples can stay in synchronicity seemingly indefinitely until the bar closes, until they finish dinner and drinks and must leave, until their train reaches wherever it is going; to put it another way, until the business of the outside world intervenes and causes their interaction to stop.'[22] However, if either partner tripped up on even just one of the above five steps (for example, not getting in synchronicity with each other), Timothy Perper and his research associates knew they could start humming the couple's swan song.

Recently, I had the pleasure of watching a couple who were obviously very much in love. I was dining in a restaurant at a table facing the bar where a young couple was sitting. Their bodies were completely facing each other, and they were leaning toward each other, practically falling off their stools. They smiled and nodded as each crooned out bits of conversation. Their hands occasionally brushed each other's and their movements were in total synchronicity as they lifted their glasses and returned them to the bar. They laughed together. They frowned together. Except for the moments when an outside noise invaded their private world, they maintained total eye contact. Even then, they turned their heads away and looked back toward each other in unison. People would say they are in love.

As I was paying my bill, the waitress noticed my watching the couple. Smiling broadly, she said, 'Yes, I've been watching them, too. Aren't they sweet?'

'Yes,' I agreed. 'They look like they're very much in love.'

'Oh, no,' she said. 'They just met ten minutes ago!'

I thought, both of them must have read Perper's Principles. Or they were, as Annie Oakley in *Annie Get Your Gun* says, 'jes' doin' a what comes natch-ur-lee!'

When You Are Quarry

The Dance of Intimacy takes two partners. Even when you are Quarry, you must remember the steps. Sadly, many potential relationships never get off the ground because, accidentally, the Quarry repels the Hunter with his or her body language.

Unlike deer or bear hunters, human Hunters and Huntresses suffer from a malady. It's called insecurity or shyness. When a Hunter or Huntress levels sights at you, you must show you are willing Quarry and be a good follower in the Dance of Intimacy.

I was once at a party with a girlfriend, Diana. An attractive man smiled at Diana, and she looked away. She confided to me, 'That good-looking guy over there smiled at me.'

'Great,' I said. 'Smile back.'

Soon after, the fellow was standing near us. I don't know whether it was shyness or a desire to play it cool, but instead of turning toward him and smiling, Diana just kept on chatting with me. A few minutes later, we saw the good-looking stranger in a warm tête-à-tête with another woman. Diana was crushed. She said to me, 'Oh, I guess he saw me up close and decided not to talk to me.'

No, Diana,' I said, wanting to shake her. 'You just didn't respond to his overtures.' She missed step one in the basic dance of lovers – turning toward him to show receptivity.

Missed opportunities like this one are happening round the clock, round the globe. Often willing Quarry crying to be captured becomes the one that got away.

The Word That Can Save Your Relationship

As you are chatting with your new Quarry, it begins to dawn on you: 'This person really is special. It's not just physical attraction. This individual has relationship *potential*.' Within thirty seconds, your heart starts pumping a little faster and your throat suddenly goes dry. Could this be the start of something big?

Instead of mission control directing all the parts of your body to make all the right moves, your brain suddenly begins wondering about the impression you are making on your Quarry. Your breath becomes short. You sense a delirious drowning feeling. Unfortunately, that is a side effect of PEA shooting through your brain.

Watch out! You can not be your engaging and scintillating self if nervousness sets in and you start thinking about your every move. There is no time now to concentrate on Perper's Principles and try to recall if *touch* comes before *synchronicity*. Or was it *turning* before *touch*? At high-anxiety moments like these, you need a simple technique to make your body do precisely what Dr Perper prescribes so you can pay attention to what your fabulous new Quarry is saying.

Hunters, the following is especially important for you because men often forget that times have changed. In the old days, a woman had to be impressed with your muscles or your speed and know you could go out into the jungle and trap a wild pig or a rabbit for dinner. However, many women today can afford their own pork pâté or rabbit chasseur at a fancy restaurant. The name of the game is no longer *impress a woman*. It's *show how impressed you are with her*.

Huntresses, most of us were weaned on boosting the male ego. Perhaps some chemical in mother's milk told us to kow-tow to all the men in our life. By age five we had already learned what worked: 'Oh, Daddykins, you're so wunderful. I know you'll buy me that Barbie doll.' Then something happened: *we grew up*. Some of us became feminists. Like throwing out the baby with the bath water, many women threw out the 'Oh, you're so wunderful' attitude along with their tattered Barbie dolls.

The modern woman feels she needs to express her capability, her independence, her superintelligence straightaway. *Wrong*! There is plenty of time to show a man these qualities later, and you *must* show them if you want to have a good relationship with mutual respect. *But now is not the time*! Now is the time to make the man feel that you think he is just absolutely, positively 'wunderful'.

Both men and women are infinitely more draw to someone who instantly likes them. In several studies, men and women who didn't know each other were told, falsely, by researchers that another participant liked them. When later questioned whom they liked in the group, practically every participant chose someone of the opposite sex who supposedly 'liked them'. Unfortunately, you don't have a researcher whispering in your Quarry's ear how much you like them, so you must demonstrate that all on your own. Since saying 'I like you' sounds a tad abrupt in words, leave it to your body to do the talking for you.

While chatting with him or her, think of this one word: *soften*. Match your body language up against the acronym which spells *soften*. It's an insurance policy against tripping in the Dance of Intimacy.

TECHNIQUE 9

Soften Your Quarry's Heart

S is for *smile*. As you are listening to your Quarry, let a soft smile of acceptance frame your lips.

O is for *open* body. Face your Quarry fully, nose to nose, belly to belly. Keep your arms open in a relaxed, inviting position.

F is for *forward* lean. Lean toward your Quarry or stand or sit just a tad too close to show you are physically attracted.

T is for *touch*. Gently, even 'accidentally', touch your Quarry's arm or brush a piece of thread from his or her clothing.

E is for *eye* contact. Remember to use all four of the eye allure techniques we discussed.

N is for *nod*. Nod your head gently in response to whatever your Quarry is saying.

'But This Is So Basic!'

After reading this segment, some of you may say, 'But this advice is so obvious! Why, in a sophisticated exploration of the complexities of love, do you suggest such mundane movements and have the temerity to call them techniques?'

For two reasons, my friends. One, because some of my most cosmopolitan and urbane friends still stumble over these simplistic steps. Two, because of their supreme importance. Research has proved that these are the specific moves that really work when first meeting someone you want to make fall in love with you.

Now let us explore two other areas where even very smart women and men mess up: the first conversation and the first date.

Chapter Ten
Your First Conversation

 ## Conversation Is Making Beautiful Music Together

Conversation is like music. Your first conversation can be a beautiful concert where all the notes fall into place, bringing joy and harmony to your Quarry's heart. Or you can inadvertently utter discordant notes that make your Quarry tune out thoughts of love.

So far we have talked about the *dance* (the body movements and choreography) to get your Quarry interested. Now, let's explore the *music* (the words and lyrics) of your love overture – your first conversation.

Think of your first conversation as an audition piece to see what role, if any, you will play in your Quarry's life. You can get away with boring interludes later in a relationship, but not now. Your first discussion has to be a smooth flow of electricity if it's going to ignite a relationship.

What is exhilarating conversation? To one Quarry, it's talking about sports, theatre, ballet. For another, it's discussing philosophy, psychology, or nuclear fission. Many people find chatting about their home, their car, or their family, dog, or parakeet to be the most engrossing dialogue by far. You need techniques to discover your Quarry's hot buttons to make sure your first conversation is memorable for him or her.

Conversation Is Like Making Love

When you are making love to a new partner for the first time, you can gently ask, 'Am I doing it the way you like? Is there anything else you want?' But you can't ask a new PLP, 'Is the conversation good for you, too sweetheart?'

When you are in bed together the first few times, you don't yet know where she likes to be caressed, where he loves to be touched. How rough does he or she like it? How gentle? You pick up hints. You watch her body, his facial expressions. You listen to her little moans, his involuntary gasps. You may sense that she goes crazy whenever you kiss her nipples. (So of course you kiss them some more.) Maybe he pulled away when you nibbled his thighs. (So you don't take any more bites on that tender tissue.)

Be just as sensitive in early chats with a new Quarry. Your first conversational interchange is every bit as important as your first sexual intercourse together – maybe even more significant, because the latter may never happen if the former isn't good.

Conversation Is Like Selling

While you are chatting, watch your Quarry's reactions to what you are saying. Keep an eye out for involuntary facial expressions, head movements, body rotation, hand gestures, and even eye fluctuations. Like a top professional salesperson, learn how to interpret all these signals and plan your pitch accordingly. With the rare exception of those who have studied the highly complex art of deception, a person cannot *not* communicate how he or she feels. Your Quarry may not say in words how he or she is responding to what you are saying, but signals are clearly telling you nonetheless.

In my sales seminars, I teach a technique I call *eyeball selling*. Knowing what turns a customer on, what turns him off, and what leaves him neutral from moment to moment can make or break a sale. Likewise, knowing what turns your Quarry on, what turns him off, and what leaves her neutral from moment to moment can make or break your relationship.

Say you have just been introduced to an exciting new stranger at a party. The two of you fall into conversation.

Watch Your Quarry's Face Throughout the conversation, his or her expression will change. Sometimes your Quarry's face will suddenly take on a lively intensity. This might occur while you are discussing something which, to you, is mundane or boring.

At other times, even when you are talking about something you consider a hot topic, his or her face falls flat. Watch for these telltale signs and tailor your conversation accordingly. When your Quarry's face comes alive, ask for more information on that topic. Keep it going. You are on a roll.

When your Quarry's face goes blank, that is your cue to gently change the subject. Move on to another topic that will bring the light back into his or her eyes. Insensitive Hunters just go on and on with a topic that is a disaster, and their prey soon wriggles out of the boring trap.

Watch Your Quarry's Head Position When Quarries get bored with you, they turn their heads away. A noise from the kitchen, someone new walking into the room, hearing his or her name across the room – any interruption will cause them to look away from you.

However, if your Quarry finds you or your conversation captivating, he or she will not glance away. An entire tray of glasses could go crashing to the floor by your feet, but your Quarry's gaze would stay fixed on you. Be sensitive to the head twistings. When your Quarry starts rotating his or her head away from you, that is another cue to spin a new conversational topic.

Explore Your Quarry's Body Position When you are stuck in boring dialogue with someone, long before you vocalize your excuse to get away, your body begins making preparations. You take a step back, and your torso turns away.

If you are chatting with a PLP who is stepping back or turning away, watch out. It could mean your budding relationship has already shrivelled up in his or her mind. However, take precise aim and give it one more good shot. Do not keep babbling on. Arrest your monologue. Use your Quarry's name. Then ask a personal question which throws the focus back on him or her. This will recapture your Quarry's attention and, if the relationship is not already crushed beyond resuscitation, it will nourish the seeds.

Conversely, suppose your Quarry is giving you a fill-faced, open, receptive body position. Top sales professionals know this is the time to move in for the close. Do the same. Make your move. This is the time to make a date, get a phone number, or suggest that you two go somewhere else and continue the discussion over coffee or a drink.

Watch Your Quarry's Hands Sometimes your Quarry's lips can lie, but hands reveal all. Occasionally glance at them while you are chatting to pick up some of the hidden thoughts he or she is harbouring.

Does he reach for a paper clip on a desk or a match on the mantelpiece while you are talking? Does she run a finger around the edge of a cup? These motions express thoughtfulness or contemplation. Your Quarry is thinking about what you just said. Take it as your cue to stop talking and let a breath of silence give cadence to your conversation. If you are uncomfortable with complete silence, at least slow down and maintain a pace that is leisurely enough to let your Quarry have his or her own thoughts.

Palms up is an excellent sign. Hunters, when she has her palms facing you, it means she likes you. She is feeling vulnerable and probably welcomes more closeness. Palms up is the classic 'I submit' position. If appropriate, now is the time to gamble a first touch, perhaps on her open palm or on her arm.

Huntresses, pay special attention to pointed fingers. Does your Quarry shake a finger in the air while making a point? Think of a pointed finger as a mini erection which shows excitement over a particular detail. If he shakes a finger in the air while making a particular point, it means he feels strongly about it. Take it as your cue to express your wholehearted agreement with him.

Keep an Eye on Your Quarry's Eyes If you see your Quarry's eyes wandering, it is not necessarily a rejection of you. It could just be that you are on a boring topic. Try changing the subject.

When you become a real expert on eye watching, you can gauge how well you are doing by the size of your Quarry's pupils. If the pupils start shrinking, an involuntary horn is blasting, 'This is *bor-ing!*' If, however, his or her pupils start growing, an internal alarm is shouting, 'I'm interested. Tell me more.'

TECHNIQUE 10

Eyeball Conversing

Don't just babble on, oblivious to your Quarry's reactions. Like a top sales pro, watch your prospect carefully and gauge your pitch accordingly. That way, your Quarry is more apt to buy your act.

How to Know What Topic Turns Your Quarry On

It is frustrating to be chatting with an attractive stranger and get stuck in the small-talk rut. You are silently screaming out, 'Gosh, I like you. I hope you like me, too. Here we are, making chitchat, but I want our discussion to be more interesting, more meaningful. What would *you* really like to talk about?'

I have developed a surefire technique to ease the transition out of small talk and on to a subject that is closer to your new Quarry's heart. I call it *cherry picking*. While your Quarry is making small talk, scoop up any unusual references in the conversation – any anomaly, any deviation, any digression, or any invocation of another place, time, or person. Pick that word out, because it is your key to know what your Quarry would *really* like to talk about.

Suppose, gentlemen, while walking home from work, a sudden rainstorm breaks out. You dart for the nearest shelter, a coffee shop. You go in, shake yourself off, and, as you sit down, you spot striking Ms Attractive Stranger on the next stool. You clear your throat and take a chance.

'Wow,' you say. 'It looks like it's going to be some storm out there, doesn't it?'

She turns towards you and seems receptive. 'It sure does.'

You are groping for something else to say. 'Erm, do you come here often?'

Your Quarry seems amused at your line, but still interested. 'No, not too often.' She smiles. 'I stopped in here for a hot coffee to get out of the rain.'

You venture, 'Yes, it's really coming down, isn't it?' Well, it might not be brilliant, but it keeps the conversation going.

'Oh, well.' Your Quarry shrugs. 'At least it's good for the plants.'

You both look out the window momentarily and then back at each other. You smile. Your Quarry gives you a forced smile. Then neither of you can think of anything else to say, so you both stare back into your coffee cups. End of possible love affair.

Rats! It started out so well. The small talk was comfortable. Your Quarry was smiling and leaning in, and she seemed receptive to you. But when it came time to get off the boring stuff and on to more interesting topics, you got tongue-tied.

Here is a quiz. In the above small talk, there was an escape hatch, a *cherry*. Ms Attractive Stranger said one word that you could have picked up on that would have catapulted you right out of small talk and into something much more interesting for her. Did you spot it?

Answer: It was the word *plants*.

Let's go back to your less-than-riveting discussion of the weather. Just before you were afflicted with that sinking 'What do I say next' feeling, she said, 'At least it's good for the *plants*.' To the savvy Hunter, that is a cue. Perhaps you wouldn't know a daffodil from a dandelion, but obviously plants are part of your new Quarry's life, or she would not have used the word. Subconsciously, even unbeknownst to her, she was crying out, 'I really prefer to discuss plants.'

TECHNIQUE 11

Cherry Picking

You will never be stuck for good discussions with your Quarry if you pick up on the *conversational cherry*. Listen for any slightly unusual word. That is your cherry seed. Plant it, and watch it flower into a memorable first conversation for your Quarry.

After she threw out that cherry, you should have asked, 'Oh, do you have a garden?' Maybe she has a vegetable garden, a roof garden, or a hanging garden. Maybe she has no garden at all but just loves plants. You don't know yet, but you do know that plants are somehow part of her world. Otherwise the word would not have slipped out.

Now suppose, instead of saying 'At least it's good for the plants,' she had said, 'I know, it's like a tropical storm out there, isn't it?' Your Quarry has just given you the cherry to save the conversation: *tropical storm*.

Say, 'Oh, have you been to the tropics?' Chances are she has, or at least has a knowledge of them, or it would not have welled up from her subconscious when discussing the rain. *Tropical*, to you, may just be a way to describe a storm, but to the person who uttered the word it has a more intense connection. Learn how to be a word detective.

Suppose she had said, 'Because of the rain my dog can't go out,' or 'Yes, the rain has been dropping leaves in my pool.' In this case *dog* or *pool* is your ticket to hotter conversation, at least for Ms Attractive Stranger.

 ## How to Fool Your Quarry into Thinking You Two Are *Already* in Love

If you eavesdrop on a man and a woman talking at a party, you could probably tell from just one minute of conversation how intimate they are. Are they new acquaintances? Just friends? Or are they lovers?

You would not even need to hear them call each other *dear*, *darling*, or *lambie pie*. Nor would you have to see their body language to work out their relationship. It would not matter *what* they were discussing, or even their tone of voice. You could just tell.

How? By the level on which they were talking to each other. There is a fascinating progression of conversation depending how close two people are. Here is how it develops.

Level One : Clichés

Two strangers talking together primarily toss *clichés* back and forth. Let's suppose they are chatting about the universally recognized world's dullest subject, the weather. Two strangers would say, 'Great weather we've been having,' or 'Goodness, this is some rain, isn't it?' That is level one, clichés.

Level Two: Facts

People who know each other but who are just acquaintances often discuss *facts*. 'You know, Joe, there were 242 sunny days last year,' or 'Yes, well, we finally decided to put in a swimming pool to beat the heat.'

Level Three: Feelings and Personal Questions

Friends often express their *feelings* to each other, even on subjects as dull as the weather. 'Gosh, Sam, I just love these sunny days.' They also ask each other *personal questions*, like 'How about you? Are you a sun person?'

Level Four: We Statements

This is the level of intimacy that very close friends or lovers enjoy. It is not clichés, and it is richer than facts. It is even more than feelings. It is *we statements*. Lovers discussing the weather might say, 'If this good weather keeps up, *we* will have a great trip.'

TECHNIQUE 12

The Premature *We*

Create the sensation of intimacy with your Quarry even if
you have just met minutes before. Scramble the signals in
his or her psyche by skipping conversational levels one
and two, and cutting right to levels three and four.

Here is a technique that grows out of this phenomenon. Use it
to make a new Quarry subliminally feel you are already a couple, already an item, already in love. I call it the *premature we*,
because you cut through levels one and two and jump straight
to three and four. Scramble the conversational signals. Ask your
new Quarry's feelings on something the way you would ask a
friend. Use *we* sentences that are usually reserved for lovers and
other intimates.

Say you are chatting with a new PLP at a party. Elicit his or
her *feelings* the way friends do. 'Do you enjoy parties?'

Proceed to the lovers' level, *we* statements. 'Yes, *we've* really
got to have a lot of stamina to get through these holiday parties, haven't *we*?'

Normally, in a budding relationship, people do not feel they
are ready for *we* statements. But when clever Hunters and
Huntresses prematurely say *we*, it subconsciously brings their
Quarry closer.

 Get Even Closer by Giving the Gift of Intimacy

Here is another conversational trick to enhance intimacy.
Usually, when talking with strangers, we keep our guard
up. We do not readily disclose personal information about
ourselves.

But, gradually, as we become more intimate with someone, we give away little pieces of ourselves like a gift. We might tell a friend or lover that we have a terrible time trying not to bite our nails, or, isn't it awful, our hair is so greasy we have to wash it everyday.

When you reveal little foibles like this to a good friend, chances are he or she will reciprocate by laughing and saying something like, 'Oh, you think *that's* bad? I go berserk keeping my hands off a zit,' or 'Your greasy hair is nothing. My barber asks me if I want a cut or an oil change!' That is how friends go on.

Such revelatory repartee creates a bond, an intimacy between friends. By sharing a secret, or making a little confession, you show your Quarry that you are not on guard. You are being vulnerable.

However, be sure you are on fairly strong footing with your Quarry before using this technique I call *early-bird disclosure*. If you sense he or she does not respect you enough yet, it can backfire. A fascinating study revealed that when a person of superior competence commits a social blunder, we like him or her more, but when a person of average competence makes a blooper, we like him or her less.[23]

Revealing a small foible is endearing. A big one is not. For example, too early in a relationship, telling your new friend that you have been twice divorced, that you had your driving license suspended, or that you got turned down by a prestigious law school could turn your new Quarry off. 'What a loser!' she might say to herself.

The facts themselves may really be no big deal. Those may be the extent of the black marks on your otherwise flawless life record of solid relationships, no misdemeanours, and a great academic record. But this early in your relationship, she has no way of knowing that. Her instinctive reaction is, 'What else is coming? If he shares that with me so quickly, what else is hidden? A closet full of ex-spouses? A criminal record? A wall plastered with rejection letters?'

Lock your closet door and save your bigger skeletons for later. Now is the time to accentuate the positive and eliminate the negative. But do reveal a tiny foible. Your Quarry will find it endearing and feel closer to you.

TECHNIQUE 13

Early-Bird Disclosure

If you sense your conversation with a new Quarry is going smoothly, make a *minor* revelation about yourself. It creates intimacy. Choose some tiny foible and reveal it like a confession, but make sure it is really minor.

Make Your Lifestyle 'Fit' Your Quarry's Lovemap

One can debate whether, as Shakespeare suggested, all the world's a stage. But it is indisputable that when an attractive stranger asks you (usually in the first five minutes), 'And what do you do?' he or she is auditioning you for a possible friendship. How you answer this question can make a big difference in what role your Quarry will cast you in. Will you be a star or just a bit player in his life?

Are you prepared? Actors prepare auditions monologues. Singers prepare audition songs. Just as experienced performers know that one song or monologue is not right for every audition, one standard answer to 'What do you do?' is not right for all Quarry. You must first size up this attractive stranger before answering, then give what I call your *Nutshell Résumé*.

If you want this new person to fall in love with you, you must consider three factors before answering this question:

1. You want to sound like the type of man or woman he or she could love.
2. You want to sound confident and enthusiastic about your life.
3. You want your answer to have a hook so your Quarry will keep talking to you.

Number 1: 'I'm the Type of Man or Woman You Could Love.'

Granted, when you first meet an attractive stranger, you know very little about him or her. But try to make your vocation or avocation in life fit what you suspect is appropriate to his or her Lovemap. For example, perhaps you sense your new Quarry wants a lover of high professional status. Make your job sound as important as possible.

Perhaps your new PLP exudes libertarian qualities. Highlight the freedom aspect of your work. He or she is a workaholic? Underscore your dedication to your job and talk about how many hours you, too, put in.

When you grasp what type of Quarry you have in your trap, feed her the lines you think she would like to hear about your work.

Number 2: 'I Love My Job.'

Everyone is drawn to confident, enthusiastic people. Women especially want a man to be confident in himself.

Once I was writing an article for a men's magazine on what qualities women look for in a man. Instead of turning to psychotherapists and studies, I simply asked all my girlfriends, 'What qualities do you most look for in a man?' Their answer? Overwhelmingly, the big turn-on was confidence. 'I like a man to be confident,' one of my girlfriends said. 'He can be a turkey – but if he's a confident turkey, it's OK.'

Men, too, like a confident woman. Often, after my friend Phil has a date, I will ask, 'How was it? Did you like her?' Phil, the typical monosyllabic male when discussing relationships, usually just mutters, 'Oh, it was OK.'

'Did you *like* her, Phil?'

'Well, yes, but I probably won't see her again.'

'Why not?'

'Well, she just didn't seem to have her life together.'

In other words, she did not have a clear and confident sense of direction about her life. Men often make that complaint about particular women.

The next time an attractive stranger turns to you and asks, 'And what do you do?' make sure your answer exudes joy and confidence about your nine-to-five life.

Number 3: 'Let's Keep Talking.'

Say you have just met the possible love of your life. You have just said, 'I'm a secretary,' 'I'm a lawyer,' or 'I'm a nuclear physicist.'

Well, that's nice. *Now* what does he say? Your one-word answer to 'What do you do?' will probably leave him tongue-tied. What do you ask a nuclear physicist? 'Oh, goodness, what have you nuked lately?'

Never just say the name of your job and let your Quarry conversationally sink. Throw him some introductory bait he can nibble on so the conversation doesn't die of starvation.

You're a lawyer? Instead of just saying 'I'm a lawyer,' expand on it. Say, for example, 'I'm a lawyer. Our firm specializes in employment law. In fact, now I'm involved in a case where a woman was actually discharged for becoming pregnant and taking some time off work.' Now you have given your catch some conversational bait. If you don't, he may swim quickly away in search of people to talk to where he feels more clever.

Sooner or later another question that Attractive Stranger will ask you is 'Where are you from?' Do more than just drop a one-word piece of geography in his lap. Prepare an interesting little hook about your home town.

For example, I am originally from Washington, D.C. When asked, I tell people that, when I was growing up, there were seven women to every man because of the influx of female government workers. (A good reason to get out, right?) With a more artistic Quarry, I tell him Washington was designed by the same city planner who designed Paris. That increases the conversational options from just Washington to city planning to Paris. The more you throw out, the better conversational hit rate you get with your new Quarry.

TECHNIQUE 14

Nutshell Resume

Whatever you do in life, wherever you go, don't blow what could be the biggest audition of your life – someone asking, 'And what do you do?'

Prepare an answer that fits your Quarry's Lovemap, is upbeat and confident, and casts some tasty bait to keep the conversation going.

Chapter Eleven
Your First Date

 ## The Game Begins in Earnest

The dance of love begins in earnest as you contemplate a date with your new PLP, but now the game is more dangerous. Starting with your first date, he or she looks at you through the eyes of an Olympic judge. Everything you say and do can give you points or ruin your chances at the gold medal, your Quarry's heart. Love is even more hazardous than the Olympics because, if you fumble on the first date, you don't get a chance to compete again next time.

Olympic skaters study for years to achieve their dream, but when they are performing, their moves appear instinctive and seemingly effortless. That is how you should appear as you build your relationship – casual and relaxed. Let me give you the scientifically proven right dating moves to win in the game of love. Study them, but when you are with your Quarry, let them become second nature so you can perform with star-quality smoothness.

'How Soon Should I Make My Move?'

Whenever one of my actress friends tells me she got the part, I can always tell from the degree of delight in her voice *how* she got it.

In the theatre there is a custom called *typecasting*. It means getting cast in a film or play just because you look the part. The traditional procedure for getting a role is going to an audition. If the producers like you, they invite you to a callback for a second audition. For big shows, there can be a third or fourth callback before getting hired.

Actors and actresses like to feel directors cast them because of their theatrical talent, not just because they looked the part. When it comes to love, people feel the same way ... especially women.

Question: How soon after meeting your Quarry should you pop the question, 'Will you go out with me?' *Answer*: Not until your Quarry feels he or she has *earned* your interest.

Gentlemen, let the attractive woman tell you of her extraordinary business acumen *before* you suggest lunch to talk about collaboration (i.e. ask her for a date). Ladies, let him tell you how much dead wood he has slashed while hacking and slashing his way through the corporate jungle *before* you invite him to lunch to meet your uncle who might employ him (i.e. wangle a date).

Let your Quarry feel he or she earned your interest or attentions through her brilliance, his fascinating personality, her talents, his wonderful uniqueness. Then she will value your company all the more. Because she got it the old-fashioned way ... she *earned* it. Let your new acquaintance pass the audition *before* you offer him the role of the romantic lead for the evening.

Gentlemen, there is another reason you should not ask her out immediately. Before she invests an evening of her valuable time in you, she wants to know she is going to enjoy it.

A woman needs more input. She needs to find out more about you. She is basing her 'go/no go' decision not only on your looks but also on your personality, your intelligence, your wit, your everything. Talk more. Reveal yourself. Give her more information so she can make an educated judgment about you before she must say yes or no.

TECHNIQUE 15 (MORE IMPORTANT FOR HUNTERS):

Let Your Quarry Pass the Audition First

Hunters, don't ask a woman out too soon, lest she think you are only interested in her looks. A woman values your interest all the more if she feels you appreciate her other qualities.

Huntresses, you can move a bit faster. Men are less accustomed to being treated as sex objects. In fact, some might enjoy it!

'Playing Hard to Get – Should I, or Shouldn't I?'

How many times have you sat by the phone offering your first-born to the monastery if only *he* would call? Once in a life time offer, God. Act now. Please.

Then the phone rings. 'Hello?'

It's him! It's him! God is good. 'Would you like to go out with me on Saturday evening?' he asks in dulcet tones.

You suppress a double back-flip. 'Would I like to go out with you? Yeeeeeeees, I would *love* to go out with you!' But you decide against that wording. You resolve to be cool because you think perhaps you should play hard to get. You hem and haw a few seconds as though you are considering his suggestion, and then you say coolly, 'Why, all right.'

Did you handle him right? Does playing hard to get pay off? The answer may surprise you.

Let's go to the studies. Four highly respected social scientists, pioneers in the study of love, were firmly convinced, as were their colleagues and the general public, that men like a hard-to-get woman better. After all, everybody values that which they have to work for, right? However, not to leave any stone unturned, they conducted an in-depth study called 'Playing Hard to Get: Understanding an Elusive Phenomenon.'[24] Researchers polled a group of college men on whether they preferred a hard-to-get woman, and why. The responses were predictable: 'Well, of course, if she's hard to get, it must mean she's more sought after. Yes, if a girl is popular, she can afford to be choosy. Well, my friends will envy me: there's a lot more prestige in going out with a hard-to-get lady.'

At this point, the researchers felt going through with a field experiment would be practically worthless. It was a foregone conclusion that hard-to-get meant better. But, being responsible scientists, they put this theory to the test. They hired a group of young men and women who had signed up for a computer-dating program. The men were to call the women and ask them for a date. The researchers told the woman that half the time, they should pause and think for three seconds before accepting the date, thus playing hard to get. The other half of the time, they should accept the date immediately, with enthusiasm, thus being easy to get.

Afterward, researchers asked the men how they felt about the women. The results astounded them. In spite of what the men had said in the hypothetical situation, in reality they did not like the hard-to-get women any better. So much for that theory.

The researchers tested and retested the hypothesis in five ways, and all five methods failed to change the result. Just as science destroyed the prevailing theories that the world is flat and that heavier stones fall faster than smaller ones, science has destroyed yet another myth: playing hard-to-get with the man does not make him want you more. At least, not at first.

But there was a wrinkle, as further experimentation showed. In another part of the study, men had the opportunity to choose from among five women for a date, thinking that other men were competing for her company. That worked. When the woman was hard to get for his rivals, but easy to get for him, he liked her more – a *lot* more.

TECHNIQUE 16

I'm Hard to Get (But, for You, Baby ...)

Considering playing hard to get? Don't ... with him. When he asks you for a date, respond immediately and energetically, 'Oh, I'd love to!' But then, later, subtly drop hints that you are hard to get for other men. Be *very* subtle.

The Scientifically Proven Best First Date

Many a Hunter, having beguiled his new Quarry into a first date, now wonders, 'Where should I take her?' Many a Huntress, when asked where she would like to go, simply says, 'Let's go out to dinner.' This has always been my choice. Over dinner you can get to know your Potential Love Partner, and it gives him the opportunity to explore all the wondrous facets of your scintillating personality.

But if your goal is get your Quarry to fall in love with you (as the fact you are reading this book attests), dinner is *not* the best choice. There is compelling evidence showing your Quarry will be more attracted to you if you place him or her in an emotionally stirring or vulnerable situation.

There is a strong link between emotional arousal and sexual attraction, as researchers proved.[25] They took female research assistants and male subjects to a scenic spot to conduct an experiment. The locale was a popular tourist attraction where the subjects could peek way down into a frighteningly deep cavernous gorge. Only two bridges crossed the gorge. One was the choice of tourists, a safe and solid bridge. And there was the *other* one. The other one was terrifying! It swayed from side to side, blew in the wind, and tipped precariously over the gorge. Only a few brave feet ever trod across this bridge.

In the study, male subjects were assigned to walk across either one bridge or the other. Whichever bridge they traversed, all males were met on the other side by a female research assistant.

After crossing the bridge, either the solid one or the tippy, precarious one, a female research assistant showed each subject a picture. He was told to write a brief story about it. Then the female research assistant thanked the subject and gave him her home phone number. She casually remarked that if he would like to 'further discuss the experience', he could call her at home.

What was this experiment all about? The researchers were looking to see which stories had more sexual imagery and which men took the female research assistants up on their invitation to call them at home.

The men who had walked across the scary bridge wrote the sexiest stories, and men who crossed the scary bridge – you guessed it – were more apt to call the females at home to discuss the traumatic experience. The experiment showed that anxiety-producing situations create a more erotic turn-on.

Why? Recall the drug we discussed earlier, phenylethylamine, or PEA. Fear produces that same substance which shoots through our veins in the early stages of infatuation.

Give Your Quarry First-Date Butterflies

Obviously it is neither possible nor practical to suggest an outing where you make your date cross a scary bridge. But science tells us, if your first experience together is stirring, your date will transfer the strong emotions to you.

Hunters, you could take her horse riding or surfing. If these physical activities are too strenuous, choose an emotionally exhausting experience – a moving play, a scary movies, or a great concert. For example, a beautiful ballet leaves me emotionally exhausted. Perhaps your Quarry is moved by music. Maybe she loves the opera. Maybe he is into watching dog racing.

Sharing anxiety and talking about a stressful situation brings couples together. Many office romances start as the two face the same challenges. Films, plays, and fairy tales are crawling with heroes and heroines defeating the big bad wolf together and then living happily ever after.

To test the findings in another way, the same researchers brought male subjects into a laboratory.[26] They told some of the men they were about to get a series of painful electric shocks. They told others that the shocks would be mild, not at all painful. While each subject was waiting his turn, the researchers introduced him to a young woman (a research assistant) who supposedly was another subject in the experiment. After letting them have a brief conversation, the researchers asked the fellows to fill out a questionnaire evaluating the woman he had just met.

Once again, the anxiety-filled fellows (those who thought they were about to receive a strong electrical shock) rated the young lady more favourably than their more relaxed brothers. This proved once again that someone is more likely to be attracted to another if he or she is emotionally aroused – even if the arousal does not come from that person.

TECHNIQUE 17

Give First-Date Butterflies

When planning your first date, find out what pulls your Quarry's strings, then plan an arousing, emotional experience. You don't have to risk life and limb together, but a little early shared anxiety is a proven aphrodisiac.

Then, of course, it is nice to have dinner afterward so you can discuss the traumatic experience.

Plant the Seeds of Similarity

Later we will explore how vital a sense of similarity is to making your Quarry fall in love with you. Now, on the first date, is the time to plant those seeds. This technique, although for both sexes, is more crucial for women because females get close through talking. Males bond through doing activities together.

Many women forget this major difference. On their first date, they suggest a place where they can talk and get to know each other. That is getting close, female-style. If you are strategically planning to make him fall in love with you, there is a better way. Suggest an activity that will bring you close, male-style. Huntresses, simply find out what activities interest him, and suggest you do that together. He gets the subliminal message, 'This woman fits in with my lifestyle.'

You may be bored to tears at the basketball game, the boxing match, or the horse race, but if that is his passion – and you want to become his passion, too – it is your best ploy.

First-Date Bonding

To plant the seeds that say you are similar, suggest his favourite interest or activity as a first date.

Remember, to a man bonding is *not* sitting across a restaurant table looking deeply into your eyes while discussing feelings – it's *doing things* together.

First-Date Restaurant Smarts

No matter what activity you choose for your first date, it's probably going to involve dinner – before, after, or as the main event. Many men dread the gruelling chore of having to choose a restaurant. Should he impress you and depress his wallet, or take you to his favourite hamburger joint?

Make it easy for him, and show him you are not a gold digger at the same time. If he asks for suggestions, come up with a great little place you think he might enjoy (read: charming but cheap).

'I Know a Great Little Place'

The way to a man's heart is through his stomach – and his wallet. In every woman's little black book should be the name of a fabulous, charming and *inexpensive* restaurant.

Men, you, too, can choose a charming and inexpensive bistro, but be aware that a first-class dinner at an expensive restaurant is an aphrodisiac for many women. There is a strong argument for taking a lady to an upscale restaurant on the first date – and not to just impress her with your gold credit card. *You* come off better in a plush setting.

Here is proof. Researchers showed pictures of men and women in various settings to the subjects.[27] They judged the same men and women to be more attractive when they were seated in a pleasant room with beautiful paintings and draperies, thus showing that people transfer their feelings about the ambience to whomever they are with.

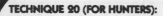

TECHNIQUE 20 (FOR HUNTERS):

Spring for a Nice Restaurant

If you are dining out on your first date, take her to a restaurant with an atmosphere like you want to project: Elegant? Upbeat? Cool? Arty? Atmosphere is important because she will transfer her feelings about the room to you.

Gentlemen, there is also an argument for taking the lady to a plush party rather than a crowded bash. The title of a study called 'Hot and Crowded: Influence of Population Density and Temperature on Interpersonal Affective Behaviour' says it all.[28]

♥ Hunters, Some Spit and Polish for Your P's and Q's

Men, I can hear you asking, 'Are you really going to muddy the love waters with talk about *manners*?' Yes, Hunters, this mud's for you. Very important stuff to a woman.

It's as good as a kiss to a woman when you stand as she enters the room, when you gently help her on with her coat, hold the door for her, or know just how much to tip the door-man when he gets the taxi. It is as arousing as a gentle caress when you suavely taste the wine at the restaurant or tell the waiter, 'The lady will have the duck à l'orange,' rather than blurting out, 'She wants the duck.'

Huntresses, men are not as susceptible to such subtleties. Unless a piece of spaghetti is dangling from your teeth or you spill your red wine all over his white dinner jacket, he will probably overlook less than flawless manners.

TECHNIQUE 21 (FOR HUNTERS):

P's and Q's

Hunters, pick up a guide to etiquette. Read it with the same intensity as you would read *How to Satisfy a Woman Every Time and Make Her Beg for More*, because when you follow the advice therein, you will be satisfy-ing two parts of your Quarry's anatomy – her heart and her brain.

Gentlemen, I suggest you go to your local library and ask for a guide to manners and etiquette. If reading such fare embarrass-es you, take a plain brown paper bag with you to tote it home.

When it becomes second nature for you to graciously take her arm when crossing the street and nonchalantly steer her clear of dog mess on the pavement without chortling, she will say to herself, 'This guy's got great technique.'

Huntresses, Forgive His Foibles

Conversely, Huntresses, if he is less than suave, don't bring it to his attention. Let the man have the pleasurable myth that he is above commonplace bloopers and embarrassing biological functions. If your date suffers the humiliation of audibly passing gas and should you wink, chuckle, hoot, or show any recognition of his biological blooper, he may return your cheap smile with a humiliated one of his own. But inside, you will lose love points.

If you are having dinner with your Quarry and he makes a faux pas, you should play the childhood game we cruelly called *Helen Keller*. Be blind to his overturned glass. Be deaf to his sneeze, cough, or hiccups. No matter how well-meaning your 'gesundheit', 'whoops', or knowing smile, nobody likes to be reminded of his own human failings.

I have a friend, Gil, now a highly paid copywriter, who came from humble origins. He grew up in the Bronx, New York. His parents had emigrated from Russia, and the family always had to struggle, so he was especially proud of making so much money and being able to afford the best in life.

Gil loved dating elegant women. When I met him, he thought he might be falling in love with Stephanie, a beautiful and, he thought, gracious lady. Stephanie impressed him because she was born with a silver spoon in her mouth and was aware of all the finer things in life he aspired to.

TECHNIQUE 22

Never Say *Butterfingers*

Clever Huntresses overlook their Quarry's minor slips, spills, fumbles, blunders, and faux pas. They obviously ignore raspberries and all other signs of human frailty in their Quarry. Successful Huntresses (and Hunters) never say *butterfingers*.

One evening Gil took her to one of the top restaurants in New York. The maître d' seated them. Gil gave the waiter their cocktail order, and he and Stephanie settled in for an intimate evening of good conversation and wonderful cuisine.

Gil took the pleated napkin off the table, placed it on his lap, and leaned in to tell Stephanie how beautiful she looked in the candlelight. He was met with a stony expression which only thawed out when the waiter arrived, removed the napkin from the table for Stephanie, and placed it on her lap.

Gil said he had no problem with table manners and social graces. In fact, he welcomed learning about them. But Stephanie's making a show of his apparent ignorance of waiting for the waiter to remove the napkin and place it on his lap put a damper on the evening. (Incidentally, it is perfectly proper to wait or to take your own napkin off the table.)

Gil tried to salvage the situation by lightly teasing Stephanie. He asked her, 'Hey, Steph, would you like the waiter to come dab your chin after each bite and ask, "One more bite for Georgie, your waiter?"' Stephanie was not amused. The evening, and the relationship, took a definite downturn.

Huntresses, no matter how lacking he is in P's and Q's, do not criticize the man you want to fall in love with you. Let the charming bumpkin blunder on through life blissfully ignorant, because even if your Quarry is sensitive to social graces, you can bet your silver spoon he is a lot more sensitive about his ego.

 ## First-Date Duds

Do clothes make the man? Do clothes make the woman? Of course not. But they dramatically influence a Potential Love Partner's *perception* of you. Remember, their perception is all they have to go on when you meet.

When I first researched the ideal love-hunting outfit, I thought (as perhaps you do now) that clothes are more important on the woman. Not so. Men's instinctive ability to 'mentally undress' a woman makes a girl wonder if it was worth spending last month's pay packet on that great Versace ensemble.

How curious it is that a woman will ruminate for hours on what to wear on a date, whereas a man grabs the first threads his groping hand hits in the darkened closet. Unless the studies lie, it should be the exact opposite. Men's hunting gear is far more important to make the kill than a woman's is.

 ## 'I Haven't Got a Thing to Wear'

(Women, Don't Worry about It. Men, Worry about It.)

Let's turn to science to get the bottom line on clothes. In a University of Syracuse study, both men and women were shown pictures of members of the opposite sex.[29] Some of the men and women in the photos wore chic up market clothes, and others wore less expensive outfits that ranged from cheap to down-right cheesy. The results?

The women were asked six hypothetical questions all the way from 'Whom would you choose to marry?' to a rather surprising scientific probing, 'Whom would you choose for a one-night stand?' How the male was dressed was extremely important to the women. Many women have an uncanny ability to spot a pair of Gucci shoes on a man a quarter of a mile away across a crowded ballroom. The better dressed a man was, the higher his marks were in all six categories – including one-night nookie.

Eventually theorists tell us that, even when considering a quickie, a woman subconsciously listens to her genes. When a man is well dressed, it signifies his ability to provide for her offspring. Even when she is wondering 'Should I or shouldn't I *tonight?*' how well you could care for her and her unborn children is in the back of her mind. Don't blame the woman. She is just instinctively doing what Mother Nature decrees.

TECHNIQUE 23 (FOR HUNTERS):

DRESS AFFLUENTLY

In spite of millions of years of sexual Revolution, men and women still approach romance differently. Even when seeking a casual liaison (i.e. a one-night stand), do not go out dressed like an unmade bed. Dress as though you were auditioning to be her husband.

Even though you know you look dynamite in your bum-hugging Levi's, with many women you will do much better at a pickup bar in a three-piece suit, even though you are the only man there so well dressed. That does not mean, gentlemen, that you can't dress casually, but forget your cheap and comfy grungies. She might find you cool in your old designer shirt, but your comfiest Woolworth's plaid polyester (which looks the same to you) won't fly high with her.

Ah, if only if it could be so simple for women. What fun to go shopping for an elegant outfit that you know will knock his socks off on the first date. Unfortunately, Huntresses, your designer suit will probably be lost on him unless *he's* a gold digger.

You can't believe he won't be wiped out by your new Oscar de la Renta suit? Believe it. The same researchers proved how relatively *unimportant* a woman's clothes are. Men were shown photographs of women prejudged to be very attractive, moderately attractive, and unattractive. The men expressed interest in having relations with the highly attractive and moderately attractive women no matter how badly they were dressed. No matter how well the unattractive women were dressed, however, overall it was a no-go. Save your expensive clothes to impress your girlfriends or your prospective employer. With men, how you carry yourself, your hair, your nails, your make-up, your grooming, your *friendliness* – that is what scores.

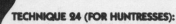

TECHNIQUE 24 (FOR HUNTRESSES):

Dress Alluringly

Women, the next time you say, 'I haven't got a thing to wear,' don't worry about it. Any outfit will do as long as it is flattering. He is going to mentally undress you anyway.

A smile, good make-up and receptive body language is far and away your most enticing ensemble.

Hunters, Huntresses, we have now got our feet wet by immersing them in the all-important firsts: first glance, first approach, first moves, first conversation,and first date.

Let us now proceed into deeper, more subliminal waters. Before we start our journey, however, I ask only one thing of you. Please suspend any preconceived notions of what you should and should not do in a relationship. Much of what you have heard is probably excellent advice for keeping a relationship warm for many years, but that is not our stated mission here. Our ambition is more cunning: it is to get someone to fall in love with you. For that, we need some of the extremely subtle techniques that follow.

Part Two

Similar Character
Complementary
Needs

I Want a Lover Just Like Dear

Old Me (Well, Almost)!

Chapter Twelve

'It's You and Me, Baby, Alone Against This Mad, Mad World'

You have heard the old chestnut, 'Opposites attract.' Mum and Dad undoubtedly told you, 'Birds of a feather flock together.' Sound like contradictions, don't they? In the magically insane, yet scientifically rational universe of romantic love, they are not.

All the studies tell us lovers are drawn to partners with similar attitudes, values, interests, and outlooks on life. In our fast-paced world of so many stimuli bombarding us every minute, our heads are spinning. We constantly ask ourselves, 'How should I feel about that? What should I believe?' With the grains of so many truths and so many lies whirling around our brains, we wonder 'What makes sense?'

Finally, when we find someone who has come to the same conclusions about the world, we feel a tremendous sense of relief. We feel close to this person. Love romanticizes that closeness into, 'It's you and me, baby, alone against this mad, mad world.'

When people construct a little cocoon around themselves and cohabit in it with a partner who feels the same way about life, it gives order to a chaotic world. They can spend their nights together in a warm womb where unknown forces and threatening values cannot assault them. Similarity makes lovers feel secure.

It is not just for security that we seek similarity. If people want long-term love, they know it is a wise choice. The studies show that similar partners have a much better chance of staying together. Similar values keep the love coals warm long after the first flames of passion have cooled.

Similarity ... and a Touch of Difference (Just a Touch)

Similarity is safe. Yet too much similarity, over time, becomes boring, so people seek differences, too. But here is the snag: they only seek *certain kinds* of differences.

Lovers want qualities that are just different enough to keep the relationship interesting but not different enough to interfere with their own lifestyles. They choose partners who can give them new experiences, expose them to new ideas, teach them new skills, improve their lifestyles, and make up for their lacks.

They also look for complementary qualities in a partner. Complementary means something that 'completes or brings to perfection'. For instance, a bashful man might be drawn to a gabby mate to make up for his own shyness. A woman lacking in worldly sophistication might be impressed with a man who knows his wines. Lovers are not looking for something different in a partner, just something different enough to fit in with their lives and bring them, as a couple, to 'perfection'.

Sometimes you hear of men and women who crave qualities entirely different in their partners. It happens. For example, a man brought up on the tight leash of a blue-blooded family might take a walk on the wild side with a street-smart woman. That street-smart woman might long for a limousine, a butler, and a maid. But, even when these two find what they *think* they want, such liaisons do not usually last long. Rarely do they result in long-term happy marriages.

How can you use this knowledge, that lovers seek similarity with a touch of difference, to make someone fall in love with you? Unfortunately, when you first meet your Quarry, you don't know enough about him. You don't have enough data to hint that, although you are similar, you are just different enough to be the right partner for her. So you must start with what you perceive. Observe your Quarry carefully. Then begin highlighting your similarities. If all goes well, you will have time later to gauge what 'different' qualities would complement his or her life.

All the studies on initial attraction establish this fact: Attraction to a stranger is a function of the proportion of similarity the subjects perceive.[30] *Perceive* is the key word here. Barring a frontal lobotomy, you cannot change your attitudes, your values, your emotional make-up, or your outlook on life to *actually* make you similar to your Quarry. You do not yet have enough knowledge about your new Quarry to even start spouting similar philosophies, hinting at similar convictions, and alluding to similar aesthetics. However, you can arm yourself with a bag of savoury subtle tricks to make your Quarry *perceive* you are similar.

In the following pages, I will arm you with verbal and non-verbal techniques to make your Quarry feel that the two of you are very much alike indeed. Some of the techniques are subliminal. Others are overt. But they all work.

Chapter Thirteen

How to Establish
Subconscious
Similarity

♥ **How to Instantly Make Your Quarry Feel, 'Why, We're Just Alike!'**

Have you ever met anyone and immediately felt, 'This person and I have a lot in common'? Instant charisma, instant chemistry, instant intimacy, instant liking.

Conversely, you might have met someone and thought, 'This individual is from a different planet!' Instant apathy, instant indifference, instant coldness, instant dislike.

Every time you meet someone, you have sentiments ranging between the two extremes. You could not put your finger on why you felt that way. You just somehow sensed it.

You probably were not conscious of it, but their choice of words had a lot to do with how you felt about them. Likewise, your choice of words exposed a lot about you to your Quarry. Our words reveal how we think. Our words peg us into one social class or another. Our words hint at our professional affiliation, our philosophical leanings, our interests, and even our outlook on life. Our seemingly arbitrary choice of words reveals how we perceive the world.

In certain European countries, there can be five or ten languages, or dialects, within the mother tongue. When two people who speak the same dialect are introduced to each other somewhere outside of their region, they practically fall into each other's arms in recognition of their similar backgrounds.

To establish similarity, you can employ a subliminal linguistic device that is easy to use but punches a powerful wallop. You can make your Quarry feel that you are part of his or her family just by your choice of words.

 ## Words to Give Your Quarry 'That Family Feeling'

Cliques of people use the same phrases. Family members and friends use the same words with each other. Colleagues in a company or members in a club talk alike. Everyone you meet has his or her own language that subliminally distinguishes family, friends, and co-workers from outside. The words may all be English, but the choices vary from area to area, industry to industry, and even family to family.

Perhaps you don't notice it, but your Quarry has a special way of speaking that links him or her to a special world of family, friends, job, and outlook on life. To give the subliminal feeling to your Quarry that you are like him or her, you can *echo* these words. All it takes is a little careful listening.

Words have different connotations to different people. You remember from school that a word's *denotation* is what it literally means. The *connotation* is all the meanings, the atmosphere surrounding it – how the word *feels*. To make your Quarry feel close to you, use the exact words he or she does.

Gentlemen, suppose you have just been introduced to an attractive young divorcée. In early conversation, she talks about her child, or maybe she says *kid, infant, toddler, tot,* or *youngster.* Probably everyone in her family uses the same word, so, when talking with her, use whatever word *she* uses to refer to the little nipper. When you echo her word, she subliminally feels a closeness to you – as though you are already part of her family.

My doctor is a young mother. During one of our early conversations, she mentioned her newborn. I knew the meaning of newborn, but it is not a word I use every day. In fact, I don't remember ever using the word newborn in conversation. But I asked her, 'Who looks after your newborn while you're working?' She smiled at me. I sensed the warmth and connection she felt with me when I used her word, newborn.

Ladies, say you are at a party chatting with a man. He is talking about his job, his profession, his assignment, or his commission. Be sure to use his word for his work. For example, if he were a lawyer, he would have said *profession*. If you said *job*, he might be put off. Whereas if the handsome stranger you were talking to were a construction worker, he would think you were being hoity-toity if you said *profession*.

Various Quarry even use different words for the places they go to work. Lawyers say they go to the *firm*, broadcasters say *station*, architects say *office*, and publishing people talk about their publishing *house*. Echoing is crucial when you are discussing someone's job or main interest because using the wrong word can blatantly label you an outsider, a know-nothing in his or her world. People instinctively tune out someone who has little understanding of their life. Since your words reveal how much you know about their world, do not inadvertently use the wrong ones.

Booking and *gig* both mean a work engagement. Gentlemen, if you are talking with a fashion model, you had better say *booking* if you want to keep the beautiful woman's interest. Ladies, if you are talking with a young pop musician, you had better say *gig*, or the dude will think you are pretty lame. If you use just one wrong word, you have struck a sour note.

Remember my PMF (platonic male friend), Phil? Once we were at a party. He was standing nearby, and I overheard him chatting with an attractive actress. She was excitedly describing a new play she had just been cast in. I heard her tell Phil that she was really enjoying the rehearsals. It also sounded like she was really enjoying her conversation with Phil.

'Oh,' Phil piped up. 'How often do you *practise*?'

Whoops! Having some friends in the theatre, I knew how that one would land. That was the last question the pretty actress stayed around for. The word is *rehearse*, friend, not *practise*.

♥

TECHNIQUE 25

Echoing

Early in a budding relationship, you don't know enough about your Quarry to invoke his values, her attitudes, or his interests. But you can hint that you feel just like your Quarry does. Simply listen carefully to the seemingly arbitrary choice of words and echo them back

♥

It is arbitrary. Naturally, actresses practise before the show opens, but stage performers never use that word. They say *rehearse*. If Phil knew so little about her world as to say *practise*, how interesting could he be to that actress?

Not ten minutes later, Phil struck again, this time in a group conversation. A gorgeous Claudia Schiffer lookalike was boasting that she had just bought a wonderful ski chalet in the mountains. 'Great,' said Phil. 'Where is your cabin?'

Her smile collapsed along with her opinion of Phil.

Dumbfounded, I couldn't resist later asking my friend, 'Phil, why did you insult her by calling her chalet a cabin?'

'What do you mean?' asked Phil, genuinely confused. '*Cabin* is a lovely word. My family has a beautiful cabin on Cape Cod, and *cabin* holds marvellous associations for me.' OK, Phil, but the shapely skier obviously didn't like that word. (Or Phil either, now.)

A new relationship is a budding flower. Uttering one wrong word can crush the little seedling before it ever has a chance to grow.

 ## 'We Even Speak the Same (Body) Language'

Happily, most people don't speak comfortably of class or social status, but there is an undeniable richness and a variety of cultural backgrounds.

Someone's background usually becomes evident after just a few minutes of talking. People with different upbringings, of course, speak differently and dress differently. Were you aware that they also *move* differently?

While travelling around the States giving talks, I occasionally cross paths with a woman named Genie Polo Sayles. Genie is a dynamic brunette who does a scandalously charming seminar called 'How to Marry the Rich'. (God bless our freedom of speech!)

Genie tells this story. Once a television crew followed her to a Las Vegas casino for an interview. The reporter grilled her on how to tell if someone was rich. 'Oh, you just know,' she countered confidently.

'OK,' the reporter challenged. 'Pick out the richest man in the casino.'

Keenly and swiftly, Genie's sharp eyes skimmed the tables. Her scanning gaze came to an abrupt halt on a young man in jeans and an old plaid shirt. With the instinct and precision of a hunting dog, she pointed a long red fingernail directly at him and announced, 'He's very rich.'

The reporter, gasping in disbelief, interrogated her, 'How can you tell?'

'He *moves* like old money,' Genie announced.

Yes, Hunters and Huntresses, there is moving like *old* money, moving like *new* money, and moving like *no* money. To capture the heart of the Quarry of your choice, move like his or her class.

I actually became aware that people from various walks of life move in different ways when I was at college. My roommate was a television junkie, and the constantly yammering box drove me to distraction. Out of desperation I bought her a headset so I could study in peace or simply savour the silence. But the flickering box had a hypnotic effect. Often my eyes would be drawn to the small silent screen. Because I could not hear the sound, I became acutely aware of how people have a different manner of gesturing, of walking. I even detected differences in how they sat down.

For instance, an actress playing the part of a well-bred or wealthy woman would first bend her knees, gracefully lower her body onto the edge of the chair, and then smoothly slide back. Whereas a Beverly Hillbilly would just plop down in the middle of the sofa.

For some people, *class* is engraved on their Lovemap. We will not address the issue of right or wrong here, nor will we delve into a discussion of how, we hope, times are changing. The Bible says 'love thy neighbour', and many people will obey, as long as their 'neighbour' is from the right side of the tracks.

For others, the wrong side of the tracks is the right side. They have no desire to get married and are much more comfortable with people from their own backgrounds. Such people are the wise ones. Studies show that marriages between people from similar backgrounds last longer and are happier than cross-caste liaisons.[31]

Straight after college, I decided to give myself a paid vacation and see the world. I took a job as a flight attendant with an international airline. Passengers called us *stewardesses* in those days. Worse, some fresh men called us *stews*, and we retaliated by tagging them *stew-bums*. My best girlfriend was another Pan Am stewardess, a spunky and attractive girl named Sandra. Together, we discovered that there were a lot of stew-bums who weren't bums at all.

We especially liked working in the first-class cabin because, on long international flights, it was very relaxed. Often, perched on their armrests or standing in the galley, Sandra and I would enjoy chatting with our passengers. On one flight, two very elegant single gentlemen were travelling first class to Paris. They asked if we were free to join them that evening for dinner at a top Parisian restaurant.

'We'd love to!' I said.

But Sandra hesitated. She ran back into the lavatory and motioned me to follow.

'Sandy, why not?' I asked her, closing the door of the john behind us. 'They seem very nice.'

'Well,' she explained, 'I'm just not comfortable around *that* type of people.'

'What, *men*?' I asked.

'No. You know,' she said. 'So, high-class.' Sandra explained that she was comfortable chatting with them as long as she was on the plane because she knew her place, but being with them in a fancy restaurant would intimidate her.

I was dumbfounded. I had not been weaned on caviar and champagne, but I had assumed that everybody would at least like to try it. Wrong! Many people only feel comfortable in relationships with people from their own background.

Incidentally, here is the ending to the Sandra story. A few months after turning down the 'high-class' dates, Sandra resigned from Pan Am to marry a fast food cook from Queens, New York.

And the last time I spoke to her, she was very, very happy.

TECHNIQUE 26

Copy Their Class Act

Hunters and Huntresses pursuing pedigreed prey should move differently from those stalking a wild cat. The polo-and-port set has a very different body language from the bowling-and-beer crowd.

Watch how he walks, how she sits down, how he gestures, how she holds her cup. Then *move* like the class of your Quarry.

Chapter Fourteen

How to Establish Conscious Similarity

 ## The Three Crucial Conscious Similarities

After you have built a sound base of subconscious similarity with your Quarry, it is time to show your affinity in three critical ways. The following similarities, or lack of them, will show up at various stages of your relationship.

Number one is conspicuous, unmistakable, and easy to create. It is what *interests the two of you have*. What kinds of hobbies, sports, and activities do you both enjoy? What kinds of music do you like, what films do you enjoy, and what books do you read?

Number two becomes evident to your Quarry gradually. It is your *basic values, beliefs, reactions, and ways of looking at the world*. This one is extremely deep. Extremely important.

Number three is subtle and elusive. It can take years to unfold, often becoming clear only after it's too late. It is also the one that is most insidious and gives couples the biggest problems in the long run. This final similarity is deeply buried, often carefully camouflaged, and seldom voluntarily revealed. To excavate it, you must sharpen your pickaxe and dig way down. It is the *tacit assumptions of what a relationship should or should not be.*

Let us explore each type of similarity. Then I will give you techniques to make your new PLP sense that you are soul mates in all three categories.

Similarity Number One: 'Do We Like to Do Things Together?'

Huntresses, beware: this one is more important to men than you think.

We will dive headfirst into the cavernous gender gap to explore it more fully later, but for now, let us look at a trite but true fact: women deepen relationships by talking together, men bond by doing things together. A woman longs for a man who understands her, whom she can talk to. She likes to feel that, when the going gets tough, there will be a big shoulder to cry on, a strong arm to comfort her, and, above all, a sympathetic ear to listen to her. Good verbal communication is important to a man, too, but it is higher on the female wish list.

A man wants a woman who enjoys the same activities, one he can have fun with. He likes to feel they can play tennis, go to concerts, basketball games or films, or just sit at home and be side-by-side couch potatoes. Doing things together is important to a woman, too, but it is higher on the male wish list. Fortunately for Huntresses it is easy to show a man this first kind of similarity. You can make him think that you enjoy his interests very early in a relationship, often in the first conversation.

My friend Phil told me about a woman he had recently met at a party. He liked her. She seemed to like him. She even hinted she would enjoy going out with him. While they were chatting, he was contemplating asking her for a date. As a prelude to inviting her to break away from the party and go to a jazz club with him, he alluded to his deep interest in jazz.

'Oh,' she said. 'I used to go to jazz clubs, but I guess I burned out on them in college.'

So much for that one.

Then Phil mentioned that the classic film *Casablanca* was playing at the arts cinema. 'Oh,' she said. 'Yes, I saw it.'

That was the end of that.

The woman may have known a lot about jazz and old movies, but she had a thing or two to learn about men. Don't cut them off at the pass. In fact, Huntresses, when you learn what interests him, hint that it is your passion, too. Many men ask a woman out just because she enjoys the same activities that he does.

I have a friend named Derek, a very good-looking man who lives in Orlando, Florida. Poor Derek is at his wit's end because he loves to jet ski every weekend. He also adores women. Because his free time is limited, he must make a choice.

Derek complains that he just cannot find a woman who will jet ski with him. You can bet the first lady who crosses her fingers behind her back and says, 'Oh, jet skiing, I've always wanted to try that,' will have a date with Derek and a head start on capturing his heart.

If your Quarry likes stamp collecting, kite flying, or going to sumo wrestling matches, tell him of your fervour for stamps, kites, or sumo wrestlers. Many men have a passion for an activity and a passion for women, but few can blend them.

TECHNIQUE 27 (MORE IMPORTANT FOR HUNTRESSES):

Ride Your Quarry's Waves

Ride your Quarry's waves. Or his motorcycle, or his horses, or his golf cart. Tell him you love donning your ski pants, your wet suit, your tracksuit, your karate *gis*, or your hiking shorts. Or maybe just your couch-potato teddy so you can enjoy a good football game on television with him.

Women want to know that, after making love, there will be something to *talk* about with their man. Men want to know that, after making love, there will be something to *do* with their woman.

Similarity Number Two: 'Do We Have the Same Basic Beliefs?'

Hunters, beware: this one's more important to women than you think.

In a university study, researchers introduced young men and women to each other and asked them to go 'have a Coke' together.[32] Before they met, some of the couples were told, confidentially, that their blind dates were very similar in their attitudes toward life. Others were told they were dissimilar. Neither statement was true. However, when quizzed afterward about how much they liked each other, the couples who were previously told they were similar liked each other a lot more — even if they were really very dissimilar. This study proved we are predisposed toward partners we think are just like us.

You have already planted subconscious seeds of similarity through the *Echoing* technique and *Copying Their Class Act*. Riding your Quarry's waves made them feel you enjoy the same activities. Now let's go for the punch right in the id, their deeply held beliefs about life. If partners share views on politics, religion, money, and possessions, it augurs well for the relationship. It is important that a new Quarry feels that you share certain values, beliefs, attitudes, and emotions and that you look at the world through the same lens. In the great scheme of getting someone to fall in love with you, it is never too early to start digging for these gems.

Women are especially sensitive to this. In fact, gentlemen, if you share just *one* strong attitude, it can spark the relationship for a woman. I have a friend, Lucia, who remembers the precise moment she fell in love with her future husband. On their third date, she and Dave were driving back to the city from a Sunday outing. After a late start, they were racing because Dave had a business meeting that evening.

Lucia's big love (before she met Dave) was animals. She works in an animal shelter and is active in the animal rights movement. Lucia told me she broke up with her last boyfriend because of one remark he made. He had said, 'Oh, I like animals, too – especially pork chops and spare ribs.'

As Dave was manoeuvring the car on a winding road, Lucia spotted a puppy lying by the side of the road. The poor pup, spilling blood from its head, had obviously been hit by a car. But, knowing how late they were and how important the business meeting was to Dave, Lucia closed her eyes and hesitated to say anything. She felt the car slowing to a stop. When she opened her eyes, she saw Dave staring at the puppy with a stricken look on his face. At that moment, Lucia knew she was starting to fall in love with him. When he suggested they stop and take the puppy to a vet, that clinched it.

Studies show it is not the number of similar attitudes that creates a deep sense of closeness. It is the intensity of one or two. Lucia did not care that Dave did not feel the same way about a lot of other things. However, animal rights was very close to her heart.

Gentlemen, do not leave an aspect this crucial to chance. Seek out a subject that is important to the woman you want to make fall for you. Bring it up. Listen to her opinions, and then wholeheartedly agree with her. In fact, give off hints that you feel even more deeply about it than she does. It is an aphrodisiac for a woman when you can intelligently discuss one or two issues that are vital to her.

It is not always necessary to have deep discussions with your Quarry to show you feel alike. In a subtle physical way you can hint at your similarity of beliefs, even during casual conversations.

Certain emotions make our bodies react in certain ways. Sadness makes us slump. Excitement causes our hands to rub together. Deep reflection makes us stroke our chin or run a finger around the rim of a glass. Timothy Perper, the singles' bar PhD, proved that the final step before two strangers became a 'couple' for the evening was the *synchronization* of movements we discussed earlier. Even if you don't know precisely what your Quarry is thinking, synchronize your movements when something happens to hint that you feel the same way.

Both men and women want partners who share their values in life. However, when a man and a woman meet, typically he is thinking more of the short run ('Will we enjoy a date together? Will she go to bed with me?'), whereas a woman has the long haul buried somewhere in her genes. The *Co-React* technique works well for both Hunters and Huntresses, but men should take special heed. Whether your imagination is forming fantasies of just a date or of a lifetime together, make sure your reactions to outside stimuli are similar to your Quarry's.

TECHNIQUE 28 (MORE IMPORTANT FOR HUNTERS):

Co-React

To capture your Quarry's heart, share his or her convictions and show you feel deeply. Watch your Quarry's reactions to outside stimuli, then show the same emotions – shock, disgust, humour, compassion.

Say you are in a nightspot and a foolish drunk falls off a bar stool. Watch how your Quarry reacts. Did he laugh? Did she show shock? Did he coolly ignore it? Did she rush over to help the drunk up off the floor?

Do the same.

Similarity Number Three: 'What Is Love?'

Couples seldom discuss the third type of similarity until it is too late. It is the most insidious because it only rears its ugly head when there is a problem.

What is this dragon that devours love? It is the tacit assumptions each partner has about what a relationship *should* be. How much closeness? How much distance? How much self-reliance? How much dependence? How much giving? How much sacrifice?

Some people feel a relationship is total intimacy and involvement. Others think it is simply loving co-existence. Some lovers agree with the French writer, Jean Anouilh, when he said, 'Love is, above all, the gift of oneself.' Others agree with another Frenchman, the author of *The Little Prince*, Antoine de Saint-Exupéry, who felt 'Love does not consist in gazing at each other, but in looking outward together in the same direction.'

Where do we get such diverse convictions of what love should be and how lovers should behave? What you expect from a relationship comes from your experience with love. The way your parents loved each other, or did not. The way previous lovers loved you and how much you liked it, or did not.

Science has dubbed your relationship expectations your 'CL', your *comparison level*. Researchers have proved that your happiness in love will be greatly determined by how far above, or far below, your CL your relationship falls. If, to you, a relationship should be total commitment and completely engulfing, a distant partner will drive you crazy. The more you try to draw that distant partner to you, the more he or she will pull away.

Conversely, if the ideal relationship to you is loving coexistence, a partner who gets too close will suffocate you. The more you push him or her away, the more you weaken the relationship.

All love relationships have a delicate balance between intimacy and independence. If the balance is off (according to either of the partners), the relationship topples. Most people are not consciously aware of the danger the disparity presents, but they have a sixth sense that it is important. People tend to fall in love with people who feel the same way they do about what constitutes love.

The next step to make your Quarry fall in love with you is to find out how he or she envisions a relationship. Then love him *the way he wants you to love him* – love her *the way she wants you to love her*. Not the way you want to love your partner.

> The single most powerful predictor of relationship satisfaction is the difference between how you think the other feels about you and how you would like an ideal other to feel about you.
>
> *Robert J. Sternberg,* The Triangle of Love [35]

Early in your relationship, start unearthing how your PLP needs to be loved. Hunters, this is a bit easier for you because women are more comfortable discussing relationship issues. If you are already close, you can ask the question outright: 'What, to you, is an ideal relationship? How would you like a man to love you?' (I don't mean sexually.)

Does she long for total intimacy and interdependence, or does she prefer loving distance? Does she want you to ask and care about her every move, or does she need more space? The answer, in all cases, probably lies somewhere between the two extremes. Try to get an accurate reading on this and all other aspects of her 'ideal' relationship.

If, however, you are not yet a couple – or if you suspect she might be uncomfortable with this question – couch it as a philosophical query. Ask her, 'How would you define love?' or 'What is your view of the ideal relationship?'

TECHNIQUE 29 (MORE APPROPRIATE FOR HUNTERS):

What Is Love?

Hunters, ask your Quarry, either directly or as a philosophical question, how she defines an ideal relationship.

Then love her not the way you think you should love her but the way her ideal partner would love her.

Gentlemen, if she appears uncomfortable even with the philosophical question, back off for a week or so. There are independent women – and their numbers are growing – who 'think like a man', or at least the way men traditionally are reputed to think. Then use the following technique which I suggest primarily for women to use on you.

Let's Talk About Our Relationship – Not!

Some contemporary relationship counsellors encourage couples to discuss their relationship openly and often. They suggest exploring their love through quizzes, exercises, and affirmations.

This can be enlightening and beneficial. But *only* if both partners enjoy discussing relationship issues, and only if both partners have the same basic assumptions of what a relationship *should* be. If the two start out with different basic assumptions, the exercises can backfire.

I have a friend, Linda, who feels a relationship is the most holy and deep commitment two human beings can make. Her parents, still happily married, are interdependent. They live only for each other and for their children. If Linda's father steps out of the house to go to the supermarket, he makes sure the entire family knows where he is going and when he will be back.

Several years ago, Linda met her fiancé, George, at a ski resort. George was different from many of the men she had met. He was self-assured and independent. He had even put himself through law school and was now a junior partner in an excellent firm. George was rightfully very proud that he had made it on his own. He had never asked anyone for anything – or answered to anyone.

Linda fell in love with George very quickly. They seemed ideal for each other. They enjoyed the same activities. They were both excellent skiers. They felt basically the same way about the important things in life. They both wanted children. They had the same beliefs about God. They agreed on how they should spend money, on where to go on holiday, and on many other issues. They wisely discussed these and other concerns before getting engaged. However, they neglected one issue, which turned out to be their undoing. George, who came from a broken family, defined an ideal relationship very differently from Linda.

Two months before their wedding, I received a tearful call from my friend. They had broken up. I was baffled. 'What happened, Linda?' I asked.

'Well,' she sobbed, 'George works very hard at his job and only wants to be with me at weekends.' She had convinced

George they should see each other more often, and he had complied. Then, on their midweek dates, he would go into long periods of silence.

'And another thing,' she moaned. 'George never phoned me when he was on the road.' She had convinced him to call her on his frequent business trips, but he had always made it seem like an effort.

Fearing their relationship was in trouble, Linda told George how she felt. He protested, 'No, no, everything is fine.' He loved her and was looking forward to their wedding. Still fearing George was drifting away, she suggested they go to a relationship counsellor. 'A *what?*' George shouted. 'No way!'

Linda was shocked. He had never before raised his voice with her. She decided on do-it-yourself help. She bought some mail-order audiocassettes on making relationships work. She listened to the tapes, which promised to help relationships by encouraging people to get in touch with their inner child. She told George how wonderful the tapes were, and she suggested he listen to them with her.

'What?' he growled. 'I'm going to take time from my work, come over to your place, light a candle, sit cross-legged on the floor, and listen to some inner brat tell me what I'm doing wrong in a relationship that I think – no, that I *thought* – was just fine? No, thank you! Linda, you've really gone off the deep end.'

The following week, George suggested they put off the wedding. I found this very sad because Linda and George had so much else in common. They could have been very happy together if only they had felt the same way about what a relationship should be. If George had the same basic assumptions about marriage as Linda had, listening to the tapes and doing 'love exercises' together could indeed have brought they closer. Conversely, if Linda had similar feelings about a relationship to George, she could have pulled away a bit and given him more space.

Generally men are less comfortable exploring relationship issues than women are, so, Huntresses, you should proceed more cautiously. Your Quarry may be gun-shy about openly discussing your relationship. If you are dealing with a man like George, asking him outright what he feels a relationship should be could put him off.

Here is a safer technique to extract the information you need. Make it non-threatening for him to open up and tell you what he expects from a relationship by removing it from the realm of the personal.

TECHNIQUE 30 (MORE APPROPRIATE FOR HUNTRESSES):

What Should I Say Love Is?

Huntresses, you *must* find out what tacit assumptions your Quarry has about relationships.

To make your question non-threatening, tell him one of your young friends or relatives (perhaps a niece or nephew) has asked you what an ideal love relationship should be. Since you don't know how to answer, you are asking his advice: 'What do you think I should say the ideal relationship is, hmm?'

Then listen. Listen *hard*.

Huntresses, thank him for his counsel. Then chisel what he says into your psyche.

One word concerning timing: don't ask about the status of your relationship too early. Wait until the two of you have reached some degree of intimacy, lest your Quarry suspect why you are asking. After your Quarry has developed affectionate feelings for you, he or she will probably appreciate the intent of your question.

That does not mean you should wait before *thinking* about this crucial type of similarity. It is never too soon to raise your antennae to pick up what he or she wants from a relationship. Listen between the lines whenever your Quarry is talking about previous lovers, parents, friends, or any relationships.

Finally comes a very big challenge. As the relationship progresses, you must do everything you can to make your Quarry feel you love him or her – not in the way you want to love, but in precisely the way your Quarry wants to be loved.

You will find more guidance on this important subtlety, including some of the right words to use, in the final two sections of *How to Make Anyone Fall in Love with You*.

Chapter Fifteen

How to Establish Complementary Needs

 'I Got Just What You Need, Sweetheart'

I remember once, as a very little girl, asking my mother what made a Mum and a Dad want to get married. She recited the following nursery rhyme to me.

> Jack Spratt could eat no fat.
> His wife could eat no lean.
> So, between them both, you see,
> They licked the platter clean.

For years, I felt that grownups always fell in love with someone who was different. On the surface I was not wrong. The studies show that, basically, men and women seek someone similar. As we have examined, lovers seek someone with similar interests, values, and ways of looking at the world and at relationships. This is the deep stuff.

However, superimposed on the similarity is a surface layer of difference. Lovers also look for complementary qualities to bring them, as a couple, to completion. Some people seek qualities to make up for their lacks. A man who can't boil an egg appreciates a good cook. A woman who doesn't know a fan belt from a fuel pump appreciates a lover who knows what is going on under the bonnet of her car. A man who can't balance a chequebook is impressed that his sweetheart knows how to read the stock market tick. Your Quarry will appreciate your complementary differences.

Maybe.

You have to be a detective and work out precisely what complementary qualities your Quarry likes and which leave him or her cold (or, worse, which make your Quarry jealous or hostile).

How do you do this? You can casually ask about your Quarry's previous relationships. 'What did you like about Jim?' 'What held you and Sue together?' 'What was Dan's best quality?' 'What was Betty's strength?'

You will hear an unbelievable variety of answers. 'Jim was so handy; he could fix anything. She always read the paper and let me know what was going on in the world. Dan was really gregarious, and we had so many friends when we were together. Betty was a super bargain hunter, so we always got the best deal for anything we bought.'

Keep your ears open and your love computer receiving data. Pretty soon a picture starts to emerge. If you have a skill that your Quarry needs (and is lousy at), you have hit gold. If you have a trait your Quarry *wishes* he or she had, bingo! That is the complementary quality that your Quarry needs in a long-term relationship.

TECHNIQUE 31

I Got Just What You Need

From time to time, casually ask what qualities your Quarry admired in his or her previous lovers.

At a later date, when your Quarry has forgotten you had asked, start hinting at what a hotshot you are in those areas.

Lovers, beware. Do not reveal complementary qualities too soon. The studies show that partners seek these assets later in the relationship, *after* they are secure in their basic similarity.[34] After you have established your similarity with the previous five techniques, this one puts the final pegs in the right holes to make you and your Quarry a perfect fit.

Let us now move on to an unbeatable recipe to conquer the heart of your choice. In the next section, we will cook up some delicious specialities to feed the ego monster and then make it become addicted to the diet you offer.

Part Three

Ego

How Do You Love Me?
Let Me Count the Ways

Chapter Sixteen

The World Revolves Around You, My Quarry

There is one conviction every man and every woman in the western world shares. That is the certitude, 'I am different. I am unique. I am special. No matter how ordinary I may appear to the outside world, inside I know I am a singular sensation.'

Some lucky children were raised in an atmosphere of unconditional love. Many less fortunate ones were not. And then there is the majority – those who grew up *thinking* they enjoyed unconditional love – only to find that there were strings attached. And Mum's and Dad's love really wasn't unconditional after all.

Many people spend the rest of their lives desperately searching for that someone who will help them recapture the childhood dream of unconditional love. They convince themselves, 'Someday, somewhere, someone will come along. This individual will recognize my specialness over all other ordinary individuals. He or she will love me for being me. Not for my physical beauty, not for my money, but for *me*, for the essence of me.'

Make your Quarry feel you are that person. Your reward is that he or she will fall in love with you.

You can make your Quarry perceive that you are the person who will give unconditional love; but you must go about it subtly. Premature, inappropriate compliments can turn your Quarry off.

 ## Ego Massage Is a Highly Skilled Craft

A skilful ego massage is not just giving compliments. It is gaining a thorough understanding of your Quarry's self-image and then fostering it. Your Quarry's ideal self-image is crucial data for planning your menu to nourish his or her ego and thus win his or her love.

Not everyone wants to feel brilliant or beautiful. There are those who want to be perceived as Mr Clean, a playboy, a Lolita, a sweet little princess, or a crazy, wonderful crack-pot genius. The variety of self-images is incalculable. The secret is not to blatantly compliment but to support your Quarry's self-image.

From your first conversation, you must listen between the lines to uncover how your Quarry sees himself or herself. The pools where people behold the most ideal reflections of themselves are the eyes of the men and women they fall in love with.

Feeding your Quarry's ideal self-image is critical for sustenance of the relationship. But it is also as perilous as handing raw meat to a ravenous lion or lioness. Beware of insincere compliments or praise that misses the mark. One bad move and early love gets eaten alive.

A well-executed ego massage proceeds gracefully through four steps. It begins with making your Quarry feel that, because of his magnetism, he has instantly captivated you. Then, as you and your Quarry are chatting, you must make him sense strong empathy flowing from you.

Step three is to start interjecting your approval. Now, as your Quarry reveals more of himself to you, you may begin to bestow implied compliments. Along the way you can develop private jokes and other techniques that we will learn to make him feel special. Finally, when your Quarry senses that you realize how special he is, he is ready for the big guns, killer compliments.

Skilled praise is a powerful magnet. People react powerfully to praise, especially from someone they have just met. Explorations of couples who broke up prove that compliments from a new admirer carried a lot more clout than those from a current lover.[35] If you are currently in a relationship, the competition is tough. Your Quarry becomes immune to many of your casual compliments and wearies of them if they are inappropriate. Taken one for one, a strong on-target compliment from a new admirer is a much more stunning blow.

The same study showed that insults and digs from current lovers, spouses, and friends are more damaging than those from strangers. Because they hold more of a capacity to hurt or offend, current lovers play double jeopardy in the game of love. This is good news for you if you are the newcomer on the scene. Use your advantage. Strike while the iron is hot. If your Quarry is currently in a relationship which is in trouble, your compliments can be a salve to soothe sagging spirits and make your Quarry turn to you for a renewed self-image.

Let us now proceed on the step-by-step plan to make your Quarry feel that he or she has, at long last, found the person with the potential to give *unconditional* love.

Chapter Seventeen

Step One: Silent Praise

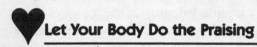

♥ Let Your Body Do the Praising

A wise sage once said, 'Love is the irresistible desire to be desired irresistibly.' When you first meet your Quarry, your body should shout, 'I desire you irresistibly. My conscious mind may not know it yet, but see how my body is responding to yours.'

Your first praise should be unspoken. You can silently praise your Quarry by showing instinctive body language deference. Upon first spotting him or her, you can even let your eyes do a subtle double take. Look once. Look away. Then let your eyes snap back as though they had a mind of their own.

While talking, maintain profound eye contact with the *intense gaze* technique. Use *Bedroom Eyes* to make your pupils grow large with appreciation. Use *Sticky Eyes* to make your Quarry feel you cannot take your eyes away – even during silences. Make sure your body focuses upon your Quarry's and that you are smiling, leaning slightly forward, and nodding in approval (*soften*).

In short, use the body language techniques we previously discussed. During this crucial initial conversation with your Quarry, make sure you maintain your own confident posture. Force any thoughts of 'How am I doing?' out of your mind. Your total concentration must be on your Quarry and your discovery of how wonderful he or she is. Your demeanour should express, 'I'm OK – and *you* are wonderful!'

TECHNIQUE 32

Body Praise

When you meet your Quarry, give the subliminal sense that you are irresistibly drawn to him or her through deferential body language.

Choose from the earlier selection of eye and body techniques to express how he or she has captivated you.

Chapter Eighteen

Step Two:
Empathy

 'I Can Identify with That!'

As your Quarry is speaking, the next step is for you to imply rapport. Let your Quarry know you understand and agree with what he or she is saying. Accomplish this by sprinkling noises or phrases of empathy, understanding, and sympathy – and occasionally your Quarry's name – throughout your conversation.

You can make simple sounds such as 'Um, hum' or a purring 'mmm-mmm'. Or you can mouth supportive phrases like 'I can understand how you felt', 'I can identify with that', 'I sympathize with you', 'I can imagine', or 'I'd have done the same thing in your shoes'. Use your Quarry's name at well-timed moments. It punctuates the conversation and serves as a potent empathizer.

Here is a conversation, slightly exaggerated, which employs empathizers and well-timed use of your Quarry's name. Let's say you are discussing tennis with a Potential Love Partner to whom you have just been introduced at a party.

QUARRY: 'No, I haven't played tennis in years. I love tennis, but I broke a couple of fingers in a car accident.'

YOU: 'Oh, that's heart-breaking [empathizer]. You must miss tennis a lot [another empathizer].'

QUARRY: 'Yes, I really do. I used to play every week.'

You: 'Oh, I understand how you feel [empathizer]. It's awful to want to do something so badly and not be able to. Have you found anything to replace your tennis?'

QUARRY: 'As a matter of fact, yes. Now I do a lot of in-line skating. And I love it – especially the speed.'

YOU: 'Oh, that's great, John [using your Quarry's name]. I can identify with that because I love speed, too [more empathizers].'

Obviously you would not use empathizers in nearly every sentence, as the overanxious Hunter above did. In moderation, however, powdering your conversation with them soothes your Quarry's ego and makes him or her want to tell you more.

A word of warning. You do not want to come across as a fawning supplicant. Good body language is your insurance policy against that. Be sure to maintain your own poise and assured body position while you empathize with your Quarry.

TECHNIQUE 33

Employ Empathizers

Sprinkle empathetic phrases throughout your conversation with your Quarry. Dust your first discussion with phrases like 'I see what you mean', 'Yes, you were right', 'I can relate to that', and the all-time favourite, 'I understand.'

Many men think, early in a relationship, they must impress their female Quarry by telling her something wonderful, unique, interesting, or original about themselves. They try to captivate her with an interesting story, an amazing fact, a hilarious joke. Even today, most men feel they must display more insights or show more knowledge to boost their status in a relationship.

No, gentlemen. Early in a relationship it is more effective by far to show empathy with her if your goal is to have her love you. Traditionally, women are not accustomed to having the focus on themselves when they are talking with a new man. Your Quarry will find you very special if you keep the spotlight on her. (Don't worry, gentlemen – you will have your chance to shine. A woman's instinct is to turn the warm rays around to you.)

In a new friendship, the smallest detail about their own lives is more interesting to most people than the most fascinating aspect of yours. That may change as you become more intimate friends, but, for the moment, your Quarry will find you more interesting if you concentrate on him or her.

TECHNIQUE 34

Keep the Spotlight on Your Quarry

Think of your conversation with your Quarry as a giant spotlight. Every time it is shining on your Quarry, he or she is engrossed. If the spotlight revolves around to you or is aimed at someone or something else, your Quarry will find the conversation (and, therefore, *you*) less interesting.

Lovers Share Intimate Details

Everyone is the star of a novel called *My Life*. Everybody feels '*I'm* special' and 'Everything *I* do is memorable.' Here is the key: People find others who share their opinion irresistible.

I grew up reading Nancy Drew novels. Nancy was the young detective heroine whose life was so exciting. So glamorous. So romantic. So *everything* my teenage life was not. Each book in the series began melodramatically: 'Nancy, her long hair flowing in the wind, raced across the moors sensing something was awry at Grandmother's house.' Wow!

In my daydreams, I wrote novels about my life: 'Leil, her braces gleaming in the sunshine, bounded into the house smelling that Mother had let a pot boil over on the stove.' Well, my turning off the stove was not such a big feat as Nancy Drew's bounding off to solve a crime, but it was *my* life, therefore exciting to *me*.

Everyone feels the same way. As your Quarry is brushing his teeth in the morning he is faced with momentous decisions like what to have for breakfast, which shoes to wear today, or whether to take time to floss or not.

Husbands, wives, and lovers share their minutiae. 'What do you want for breakfast, dear? You're not going to wear *those* shoes, are you? Did you remember to floss?'

Obviously, when you meet a new Quarry, you cannot feign interest in what she had for breakfast or whether he flossed or forgot. But you can create another immediate intimacy. Simply make a point to remember the intimate details of her life.

Clever Hunters cater to their Quarry's craving to be a star through a technique I call *tracking*. Just like air traffic controllers track aircraft on their radar screens, clever Hunters track the verbal traffic of their Quarry. If, in early conversation with your Quarry, he mentions he had Rice Krispies for breakfast, allude to it later. If, in chatting, she tells you she wore mismatched shoes to work one day, find a way to let the subject come up again later. It shows she is a memorable star in the galaxy of people you have met. Over time, such trifling pebbles meld to form rocks of intimacy.

As a relationship goes on, wise lovers keep a mental little black book of their Quarry's last concern, last enthusiasm, last conversation. They keep track of where their Quarry went, what their Quarry said, and what he or she was doing since they last spoke. When they talk again, the *first* words out of their mouth, either on the phone or in person, refers to it: 'Joe? Hi! How did your meeting go? Hello, Linda. Has your sister had her baby yet? So, Jim, did you survive that Szechuan restaurant you were going to last time we spoke? Diane, how's your toothache now?'

TECHNIQUE 35

Tracking

Like an air traffic controller, track the tiniest details of your Quarry's life. Refer to them in your conversation like a major news story.

When you invoke the last major or minor event in anyone's life, it confirms what they have known all along. They are the leading character in that riveting novel, *My Life*. They will love you for recognizing their stardom.

Let your Quarry feel that *minor* events in his or her life are *major* concerns in yours.

 Lovers Have Private Jokes

Here is another delectable way to milk your Quarry's ego and squeeze out the first drops of love, even before it's suitable to give a full-blown compliment.

Happy, intimate couples share private jokes. They whisper phrases in each other's ears that mean nothing to anyone in the world but themselves.

With no lengthy explanation, playwright Neil Simon can make an entire Broadway audience understand that two performers on stage are either married or longtime lovers. Simon has the performers exchange a few words which make no sense to the audience, then both of them crack up. The audience gets the message: these two people are an item. You can create a similar impression of intimacy with your new Quarry. Simply find a private joke shared by just the two of you.

Here is how to set it up. Whenever your new Quarry is telling a story, either to you or to a group, remember some part of it that he or she obviously delights in. Then weave a phrase, a little joke, that invokes your Quarry's favourite part.

Occasionally, I go out with an English chap named Charles. When I first spotted Charles at a party, he was telling a group of friends about his hiking trip in the mountains with several other men. A few hours into their expedition, Charles told us, they came upon a steep mountain covered with loose falling rocks. He and his mates did not want to scale the dangerous terrain, but of course none of the macho men, including Charles, would admit they were afraid.

Charles happened to have a large thermos of hot tea in his backpack. As the brave hikers stood there gazing up at the peak sceptically like frightened little boys, Charles made a suggestion. In his terribly British accent, he proposed, 'Oh, do let's have a cup of tea first.' Great idea! Everyone dived for a seat. As they squatted on the rocks gulping tea, they planned an alternate, safer route.

Charles didn't say it in so many words, but the unspoken point of his story was that he, Charles, had saved the day and, possibly, their lives by his line, 'Oh, do let's have a cup of tea first.'

Later on in the party, Charles suggested the host turn on the television to catch the end of an English rugby game being broadcast that evening. Everybody at the party thought that was a *terrible* idea. I winked at Charles and said, 'Oh, do let's have a cup of tea first.' He cracked up. I think that was the first time he noticed me.

TECHNIQUE 36

Private Joke

To create premature intimacy, listen carefully while your new Quarry is telling a story. Then pick out a phrase that he or she obviously relishes. Caption this favourite passage and repeat it back to your Quarry later in the conversation to make him or her feel very special. You now share a private joke, just like longtime lovers.

As with all sensitive communcation techniques, you must heed a few cautions. Caution number one: only choose events where your Quarry shines – where he or she was the hero of the story, not the buffoon. Some people tease their friends about the time they spilled the drink, lost the keys, cracked up the car, or slipped on the banana peel. That is called *heckling*, and it has the opposite effect.

Caution number two: after you hear your Quarry's story, let some time pass before you invoke the private joke for the first time. The longer the interval, the stronger the punch.

Not only does creating a private joke with a new Quarry work wonders for giving a relationship liftoff, it also softens rough edges that surface later on. To this day, whenever Charles comes up with a suggestion I don't like, I simply say, 'Oh, do let's have a cup of tea first.' He laughs every time. Charles enjoys my story so such that he forgets I am disagreeing with him, and I usually get my way.

Chapter Nineteen

Step Three: Admiration

 'Oh, Darling, You Did an Absolutely Superb Job Slicing These Mushrooms'

Step three, in early conversation, is to convince your Quarry you admire him or her. Now is the time to add reinforcing statements to express approval. These little interjections are called *kudos*. Let's say your hypothetical conversation now turns to jobs.

QUARRY: 'Yes, I really got tired of that job, so I decided to quit.'

YOU: 'Mmm, you made a courageous move [admiration].'

QUARRY: 'Yes. Well, then I took some night courses to brush up on accounting.'

YOU: 'That was wise [approval].'

QUARRY: 'Well, I thought so.'

YOU: 'Have you had the chance yet to use your new skills?'

QUARRY: 'I sure did. It landed me a job with my present firm.'

YOU: 'Wonderful, John! [using your Quarry's name] It must be a good feeling to know that you made the right choice [empathizer].'

As the conversation progresses, keep weaving in kudos and empathizers. Remember, kudos are *not* full-blown compliments. They are simply little empathetic commendations such as: 'I can see you really worked hard for that cause. That's great', 'Sounds like you had a good handle on that situation. Congratulations', 'You said *that*? Not many people would have had the guts', or 'You really did that? Gosh, that's impressive.'

Hunters, giving kudos may be harder for you than for women. Men, who are more competitive by nature, sometimes feel that giving compliments diminishes their own rank. On the contrary, the more popular and secure a person is, the more apt he is to give reinforcing statements. Praising others enhances your own rank.

Additionally, women do not see compliments in terms of rank. For them, praise deepens intimacy. When you give a woman kudos, you will stand out from other Hunters. It is a rare man, indeed, who expresses admiration for the accomplishments of a woman he has just met.

Huntresses, you can be downright profligate with your kudos. What may sound like blatant fawning to you will sound perfectly logical to your Quarry's ears.

I have a half-brother, Larry, who recently married a charming older woman. A few weeks after their wedding, I invited them to dinner. Larry is a fine chef, and Regina and I decided we would be his *sous chefs*. The three of us scurried around the kitchen. Regina was peeling onions, Larry was slicing mushrooms, and I was putting some water on to boil. At one point, as I was leaning over the stove, I heard Regina purring to Larry behind me, 'Oh, darling, you did an absolutely superb job slicing these mushrooms. Just look at how evenly and cleanly you cut every single one.'

I turned around to share a big smile with Regina at her joke, but she wasn't joking! Regina was earnestly admiring his tiny mushroom slices. Larry was the one who was smiling – actually beaming – with pride.

Regina, it dawned on me at that moment, is a very smart woman. She knew Larry prided himself on his careful kitchen work. I'm sure Regina's unblushing use of kudos was one of the reasons my half-brother fell in love with her and will probably stay that way forever.

TECHNIQUE 37

Confer Kudos

As the intimacy progresses, add approval notes to your empathizers. Sprinkle your conversation with little phrases like 'Good going', 'Not bad', and 'That was smart.'

Huntresses, don't be bashful. Men eat it up. Hunters, force yourself to give kudos. It is a new skill for you.

Chapter Twenty

Step Four: The Implied Compliment

'You're Much Too Young to Remember This, But ...'

Here is yet another way to puff up your Quarry when your relationship is still too fragile to hold a full-blown big compliment. *Imply* that your Quarry is wonderful in the 'incidental' part of your sentence. Implied compliments are phrases like, 'You're too young to remember this, but ...' or 'Anybody as good-looking as you wouldn't ...' You are praising your Quarry, but not directly.

You have a choice. You can couch the implied compliment in the dependent clause of your statement, such as, '*Being as smart as you are*, you wouldn't fall for a scheme like that, but I did,' or '*Anyone as well spoken as you* could easily get straight through to him on the phone.'

Another way to craft the implied compliment is to insinuate your Quarry is part of some exceptional group. Say something like '*Really bright people like you* often feel that way' or '*Anybody as fit as you are* could do it with no problem.'

You can make liberal use of the implied compliment, because it does not appear as though you had the intention to flatter. Your exalted opinion of your Quarry, well, just slipped out.

TECHNIQUE 38

The Implied Compliment

Pave the path to your Quarry's heart by tucking implied compliments into the secondary parts of your sentences.

You can also hint at your exalted opinion of him or her by referring to your Quarry as part of some superior group.

The Bull's-Eye Booster: 'I Just Love What You Like About Yourself'

Most people praise their Quarry for something they like about him or her. But is it much more potent when you compliment your Quarry for something he or she is really proud of.

Early in your conversation, start consciously gathering booster material. Carefully craft your praise so it darts directly, dead centre, into your Quarry's heart. This takes some careful listening with a psychiatrist's ear. While your Quarry is talking, watch his or her face. Be on the lookout for cheeks blushing, eyes brightening, smiles flickering. These expressions are gifts to you – gifts of revelation of what turns her on about herself. When his face becomes lively, it means he is enjoying what he is telling you. If it becomes bland while she discusses a particular accomplishment, don't bother to compliment that one.

Recently, I was having lunch with a charming, but rather chauvinistic, business associate named Ralph. Just that morning, Ralph had given a speech to a group of female business executives. Before the speech he feared the feminists in the group would eat him alive. As he told me the story, his eyes began to sparkle. With great animation he related the 'man-bashing' joke he opened his speech with to win the crowd over.

Later, at the same lunch, Ralph told me another story. This second one was truly impressive. He told me how, from humble stockroom-boy beginnings, he quickly rose to become president of his company. During this tale, Ralph's face was bland, unmoved.

Which accomplishment do you think Ralph would most like to be praised for? Yes, even though in real-world terms the latter is far more praiseworthy, winning over his potentially unfriendly female audience was Ralph's conceit. If, by chance, you wanted to win over his chauvinistic heart, you would say, 'Oh, Ralph, that was clever of you to open with that joke.'

Before delivering your first overt compliment, reflect on your Quarry's self-image. Where does her vanity lie? What would he most like you to recognize him for? Does she fancy herself extremely bright? Absolutely gorgeous? A spiritual person? Does he fancy himself a lady-killer, a shrewd judge of character? A wild, funny, rakish kind of guy? Maybe she is proud of her hilarious sense of humour, her deep sense of honesty, her creativity. Or, like Ralph, he is proud of his ability to win feminists over through clever wit. Analyse what your Quarry is most happy about in himself and then praise that.

Often an attractive woman would prefer you to praise her intelligence and insights than her appearance. An accomplished man, weary of hearing how bright he is, might respond more warmly to your telling him how good-looking he is. The more your praise conforms with your Quarry's ideal self-image, the more he or she will appreciate it.

Hunters and Huntresses, when praising your Quarry, also consider timing. Praise for a recent small victory carries more punch than applauding a greater, more distant, feat. Complimenting someone's new outfit is best on the day he or she bought it. In this case, Ralph liked being complimented on his man-bashing joke victory because it happened that morning, whereas his meteoric rise had taken place decades ago.

TECHNIQUE 39

The Bull's-Eye Compliment

Before you fire your first overt compliment, ask yourself, 'What is this person most proud of?' Then take precise aim.

Also consider timing. You warm your Quarry's heart more by praising a new achievement over an old.

Chapter Twenty One

Step Five:
The Big Guns

 ## 'You Are the Most Fascinating Person I've Ever Met'

Each time you discharge an obvious compliment, your next shot loses power. Like the old pound notes, your Quarry begins to devalue conspicuous compliments. You can use empathy, make approval noises, and imply your praise early with your Quarry. But save up for the *killer compliment*.

What is the killer compliment? It's not, 'Gosh, I like your tie.' A killer compliment is a knock-'em dead, on-target, out-right compliment which takes your Quarry's breath away.

In my communications seminars, I trick people into killer complimenting another participant. Early in my programme, I ask the participants to get to know another participant by chatting for a few minutes. Later in the programme, I instruct them to close their eyes and recall one outstanding positive quality about the person they spoke with. I say, 'Not anything you would necessarily *tell* the other person, but some very private positive observation about them.' Perhaps their conversational partner had a wonderfully warm smile or there was a spiritual air about them. 'The quality can be physical,' I tell them, 'or it can concern their personality.' Everybody has at least one good quality.

Then I say, 'OK, now, open your eyes, and tell them what you were thinking.'

'What, *tell* them?' They are in shock. 'Actually *tell* the other person the private thought I was having about them?'

'Yes! Tell them.' I remind them that I said to think of a compliment that they would not *necessarily* tell the other person.

They give each other killer compliments, and the result is a joy to watch. After the first wave of nervous laughter sweeps the crowd, smiles and warm blushes break out all over. Friendships are forming right and left. Everybody enjoys receiving their killer compliment, and practically everybody develops warm feelings toward the person who gave it to them.

What kinds of killer compliments have they just heard? Lovely sentiments like: 'You have a terrific sense of humour', 'What penetrating deep brown eyes you have', 'I thought you were a dancer. You move so gracefully', 'I noticed your hands. They're like a pianist's'. 'I sense an aesthetic quality about you', or 'I love your teeth!'

 ## 'What Does Giving a Killer Compliment Do for Me?'

I'm sure you have worked out by now that giving the killer compliment is not an entirely altruistic act. You receive a rich reward yourself when you candidly blurt one out.

Recently, at a party, I was chatting with an accountant, a dull one at that. (Apologies to accountants everywhere who must battle the unfair dull, pencil-pushing, green-sunglasses wearing, number-crunching image!) As I was trying to break away from the tedious accountant, he looked deeply into my eyes and said, 'Leil' – he used my name – 'you are the most fascinating woman I've ever met.'

Whoa! Stop! Time out! My knees got weak. (Did I sense a little PEA shooting through my veins?) 'Who *is* this man?' I thought. Suddenly the fellow became very interesting. In fact, I wound up having a lunch date with him the next week.

As it turned out, the chap truly was dull, and the relationship went nowhere. But his killer compliment gave our relationship the best possible shot it had.

TECHNIQUE 40

The Killer Compliment

Search for a unique quality in your Quarry, one so deep that most people would not comment on it.

Then look your Quarry straight in the eye, use your Quarry's name, and knock his or her socks off with the killer compliment.

Just as black-belt karate grand masters register their fists as lethal weapons, killer complimenters should register their tongues as lethal weapons in making the kill with their prey. The killer compliment is such a mighty missile, it should come with a user's manual. The user's manual would tell you to shoot out your killer compliment in one strong, sharp sentence, eyeball to eyeball. If it goes on too long, you will embarrass your Quarry. Deliver your killer compliment upon parting, as it will leave your Quarry speechless and only able to stammer, 'Oh, gosh, thanks.' (Don't worry, he or she will be back for more.)

Obviously, don't give more than one killer compliment to your Quarry in a given month. Otherwise, you come across as obsequious and pandering. As in all compliments, make sure it is about something the recipient is proud of.

One time I was in a small play in which I portrayed eight different characters. I smugly thought, 'What a flexible actress I am.' The least impressive role, in my opinion, was when I portrayed a department store mannequin. In that skit, another actor did all the performing while he carried me around the stage like a frozen corpse. Sometimes a gushing audience member would come up to me after the show, grab my hand, and say 'Oh, I loved you in that mannequin scene.' How I hated that! Do you believe I developed hostile feelings against such well-meaning flatterers?

Make sure your praise supports your Quarry's self-image. Otherwise it backfires. For example, if you say to an actor, 'It's wonderful how you memorized all those lines,' or, to a dancer, 'You looked so pretty in that costume,' you have actually insulted their performances. Your well-intended praise goes kerplunk, and kerplunk compliments do nothing to ignite love.

Armed with these nine ego-massaging techniques, go forth now and capture your Quarry. Before using them, however, you must ask yourself one final question: 'How susceptible is my particular Quarry to praise?' Let's explore that.

Chapter Twenty Two

Fine-Tuning the Ego-Machine

 'Wait a Minute. Does *Everybody* Like Compliments?'

A dollar means less to a millionaire than it does to a pauper. And a compliment means less to someone who is used to being praised. If you are tracking extremely attractive Quarry or very accomplished Quarry, you must work harder and be more original in your compliments. Such people are accustomed to being admired, so they pooh-pooh early praise.

A study showed that, although attractive people tend to discount early praise, physically less attractive people value it much more.[36] In fact, they are ravenous for your compliments. Trapped inside every plain-faced woman is a beautiful enchantress crying to be set free by your making her feel beautiful. Trapped inside every frog-faced man is a handsome prince waiting for you to kiss him with praise.

TECHNIQUE 41

Short on Assets? Go Long on Praise

Attractive and accomplished people are accustomed to praise, so compliments often have less value on the open market. Seek original praise for popular Quarry.

However, if your Quarry is not used to being praised, he or she is hungry for your words of appreciation, no matter how trite.

Feed your Quarry's ego the *appropriate* diet and watch his or her love grow.

Knee-Jerk Praise: 'What You Just Did Was Fabulous'

Here is a little pistol shot you *must* use with everyone whether her face is plain or pretty, whether his accomplishments are trivial or triumphant. I call it the *knee-jerk compliment*.

There are crucial moments when, if you *don't* offer a compliment, you will offend your Quarry. If he or she has just finished an accomplishment (made a big sale, taken a final bow after a performance, successfully negotiated a deal, cooked a great meal), make sure the very first words out of your mouth relate to that just-completed triumph. At that moment, your Quarry is sure to have only one raging question in his or her mind: 'How did I do?' If you don't want to lose love points, you must first give your Quarry an instantaneous knee-jerk compliment.

A friend once told me how disappointed he was in his girlfriend's reaction to a speech he gave for his industry's convention. Straight after his talk, which had been a great success, he strutted back amidst the applause to take his seat next to his significant other. The first thing she said to him was,

'Wave to Bill and Sue back there. We didn't know they were going to be here.' Boom! What a letdown. Where was his well-deserved compliment?

A few moments later she did say, 'You gave a great speech, sweetie,' but it was too late. What a difference if she had first complimented his speech and then said, 'By the way ...'

TECHNIQUE 42

The Knee-Jerk Compliment

After your Quarry's accomplishment, compliment *immediately*. The first syllables you utter must be the flattering answer to the unasked question, 'How did I do?'

One last caution on the knee-jerk compliment. Be sure your compliment shoots high enough. When in doubt, aim even higher. 'Good job' might come across as insulting if he thought he had done a *great* job. 'Nice presentation' could be a real disappointment if she thought she had made a *terrific* presentation.

 Have the First Laugh

To a comedian, your face is just one of many bobbing around in the sea facing him in the club. As he delivers each punch line, you suspect he is unaware of who starts the trickle, or the riptide, of laughter.

Not so! As a speaker, I guarantee you that every one of my colleagues knows precisely who inaugurated the laughter, precisely how long after the punchline was delivered, and precisely how enthusiastically they laughed.

Huntresses, so it is with most men, even if they are just telling a joke to a few friends.

TECHNIQUE 43 (ESPECIALLY FOR HUNTRESSES):

Have the First Laugh

Huntresses, it is with embarrassment that I offer you this obvious technique, but leaving it out would be a grave sin of omission.

Be the first to laugh at his jokes, and laugh the longest. Many a Huntress who had the first laugh when her Quarry made a joke has had the last as she waltzed off to the altar with him.

Lovers Give Each Other Pet Names

By now you are ready for another tender trap to create intimacy with your Quarry and make him or her feel like the centre of the universe.

Many of us, when we were children, had nicknames. Lots of today's Roberts were once called Bobby. Many Elizabeths were once little Betsy. Many Johns were Johnny, and Sues were Suzie. Did you have a nickname? I did. My mother and all the other kids called me 'Leilie'. That remained my official designation until I decided it wasn't respectable-sounding enough for the young professional I aspired to be. So, along with my intended personality change, came a name change. I insisted everyone call me Leil.

I have one friend from my childhood days, Rick, who resisted the change and to this day calls me Leilie. Whenever I hear a voice on the phone asking to speak to Leilie, my heart thumps with childhood memories. The emotions that I feel upon hearing *Leilie* get transferred to Rick, and I am sure the fact that Rick (I call him Ricky) calls me Leilie is one factor in our friendship lasting so long.

Childhood experiences and childhood names have a strong subliminal effect. Like any weapon, however, this one could backfire. If your Quarry had an unhappy childhood, hearing an old nickname might invoke horrible memories. If Walter's parents were always dumping on him, your calling him Wally could drive him up the wall. If Elizabeth was a battered child, just the name Lizzie could make her go bonkers. Test market the pet name on your Quarry first.

However, if your Quarry had a happy childhood, using a pet name deepens intimacy, and it shoots a little PEA through his or her veins every time you say that name.

TECHNIQUE 44

Confer Pet-Name Status

If it is appropriate, ask your Quarry what he or she was called as a child. If you sense that your Quarry likes that pet name, say, 'Oh, I love it! Do you mind if I call you that?'

When Your Quarry Praises You

One day I was browsing in a bookstore for a book on compliments. Nowhere to be found! But there was a big fat one of several thousand insults, 'for all occasions' it proclaimed. It was full of supposedly hilarious insults like, 'Hey, you're so ugly you have to have your x-rays retouched,' or guaranteed lines like, 'You look much better without my glasses.' Guaranteed yes, to get you a cheap laugh, but not to make someone fall in love with you.

Many of us, even if we would never dream of delivering a hackneyed line like that, still inadvertently insult our Quarry when he or she compliments us. We are often beastly at giving compliments – and receiving them. It's a national characteristic. They simply stammer a weak thank-you. Worse, they say, 'Oh, it was just luck.'

This lukewarm reaction does nothing to make your Quarry feel good for complimenting you. Furthermore, if you mumble 'Not really' or attribute your success to 'luck', you are indirectly insulting your Quarry's powers of perception. After getting no positive feedback, your Quarry will quit complimenting you.

Whenever your Quarry praises you, don't just say, 'Oh, shucks,' or even, as Amy Vanderbilt suggests, 'Thank you.' Go Amy one step better. Reflect the sunshine of the compliment right back on the giver. Quickly murmur, 'That's very kind of you,' or 'How sweet of you to notice.' The French do it regularly. Instead of saying *merci* (thank you), the gracious ones murmur '*C'est gentil*' (loosely translated, 'That's kind of you').

If someone hurls a boomerang, it does an almost 180-degree turn and comes right back at the thrower. I call the technique of reflecting the compliment back *Boomeranging*. Here are some examples of boomeranging: How's your family? 'Oh, they're fine. *Thanks for asking.*' How was your holiday? '*Thanks, you remembered*! [Show you are obviously impressed that they did.] Yes, I really had a great time.' I really like your new hairstyle. '*Oh, thanks for noticing.* Yes, I found a great new hairdresser.'

TECHNIQUE 45

Boomeranging

When your Quarry compliments you or asks you about anything you enjoy talking about, boomerang the good feelings back.

Thank him or her for asking or noticing. Stamp out childish embarrassment and let your big smile show your Quarry you appreciated the compliment.

When you *boomerang*, your Quarry will feel good for having praised you. Human animals, ever in pursuit of good feelings, will conjure up some more good thoughts about you to make themselves feel good. The more good thoughts your Quarry has about you, the more twigs it puts on the fire of love.

Chapter Twenty Three

Keeping the Love Coals Warm

 'I Love the Way You Wrinkle Your Nose When You Laugh'

This final ego-massage technique concerns long-term love. It helps keep *you* in love with your Quarry because it keeps your Quarry doing the things you love. Love is a two-way street, and it is hard to keep someone high on you if your affection for them sags.

Dr Benjamin Spock is the famous baby doctor who in the 1950s taught American parents how to cope with their off-spring. Today, controversy swirls around his doctrine of permissiveness, but the well-intended doctor leaves the world with at least one good axiom. He said, in essence, 'Tell the little tyke that he is great, and it will encourage his greatness.'

I call this technique *Spocking* after this baby philosophy. *Spocking*, on an adult level, is doing the same with your significant other. Divulge what you love, appreciate, or admire in your Quarry so he or she will keep doing those things you love, appreciate, or admire.

People start to fall in love for a myriad of different reasons. The logic, flowing from your Lovemap, can seem as arbitrary as loving the way she wrinkles her nose when she laughs or adoring the way he caresses your cheek. You might have fallen in love with him when, the first time you invited him to dinner, he washed the dishes. You might admire her strength in the face of crisis or respect his sense of honesty.

To stay in love (and therefore keep your Quarry in love with you), encourage that which you adore. Say 'I love the way you wrinkle your nose when you laugh.' Say, 'It's so exciting when you caress my cheek.' Say, 'Believe it or not, one of the things that I really love about you is the way you offer to do the dishes.' Say, 'I admire your strength in the face of crisis.' Say, 'I respect your deep sense of honesty.'

I remember a lovely *New Yorker* cartoon, so poignant I cried. The drawing was of an obviously poor, overweight, and exhausted couple sitting at their kitchen table. The husband, in his T-shirt, had not shaved. The wife had curlers in her hair. Dirty dishes and nappies hung on a makeshift clothesline strung from a pipe to the fridge. They were drinking coffee out of chipped old mugs.

The caption was the man smiling at his wife, saying, 'I just love the way you wrinkle your nose when you laugh.' The couple looked genuinely happy, in spite of the mess, in spite of their poverty, in spite of their exhaustion. If *Spocking* was part of their daily life, they probably were.

♥

TECHNIQUE 46

Spocking

Think about the subtle, maybe even silly, things you love about your significant other. Then, at odd moments, tell him or her what those things are.

Your partner is not a mind reader. More than just saying 'I love you', you need to tell *why*.

♥♥

Many people neglect to tell their significant other what *really* turns them on. (Yes, this applies to sex, too.) The significant other, not realizing its importance, stops wrinkling her nose, caressing your cheek, or washing the dishes. Then one tiny bulb goes out in the magnificent array of glimmering lights that make up love.

If other bulbs start burning out one by one, the love can go dark. If your significant other becomes insignificant to you, you are both losers. Keep *Spocking* the qualities in the ones you love to keep the love alive.

Part Four

Equity

The 'WIIFM' Principle of Love
(What's in It for Me?)

Chapter Twenty Four

Everybody's Got a Market Value, Baby

During a heated argument, a man I once loved snarled at me, 'Everybody's got a value on the open market, baby.' I was appalled. How crass! How could he see people as commodities, especially somebody he said he loved? What a repulsive way to look at relationships!

To me, love was beautiful. Love was pure. It was the source of the most intense pleasure known to mankind and had no parallel in human experience. To me, love was sharing, trusting, total giving of self. The words of Robert Burns had reverberated in my heart since childhood: 'Love, O lyric Love, half angel and half bird. And all a wonder and a wild desire.' To hear my lover liken his loved one's qualities to pork bellies or soybeans on the commodities market was too much. I stormed out of the room. And, soon thereafter, out of the relationship.

Now, many years later, older and, some few could argue, wiser, I wonder, 'Was he right?' Not in his manner of presentation, certainly. But in his facts? It surprises no one to hear, 'Everyone wants to get the best deal possible in life.' Nor are they shocked when they learn about the law of supply and demand in business. People don't even flinch when sales gurus preach that, in all human interaction, the big question is WIIFM – (what's in it for me?)

Why do we recoil when researchers tell us the same natural laws apply to love?

Recently, the scientific community, not content with the theories of love proposed by Sigmund Freud (sublimated sexuality) or Theodore Reik (filling a void in oneself), set out to get the real low-down on love. Conducting numerous surveys and laboratory experiments, scientists peeled back a deeper layer of the human psyche. Did they uncover some ugly facts? Did they confront a monster? Some might say 'yes'. Others would laugh it off and say, 'Of course not.'

Whether you see their findings as the abominable snowman or the archangel of truth, the result is quite simply this: studies do indeed support the thesis that everything and everybody has a quantifiable value on the open market. And everybody wants to get the best deal possible in love as well as in life. Researchers christened their findings the *equity* (or *exchange*) theory of love. It is sort of like the old *horse-trading principle*.

 ## Why Is Finding Love Like Horse Trading?

The equity theory of love is based on the same sound business principles of barter and open market value. Everything has a value. Everything has a price. As with that of a product, a person's value can be subjective. Generally, the world agrees on what is a good catch and what is a shoddy one.

In the world of horse trading, there are *top-grade champions* or *nags* (horses ready for the glue factory). At a horse auction, buyers look for qualities they describe as *pretty movers, good disposition, no bad vices*, and even *flashy*. Are humans really so different?

All these horse qualities affect the sales price. If you are trading a registered horse for one without pedigree papers, he had better have some of the other superior qualities to make it a fair barter.

Studies show that the more qualities you bring to the bargaining table, the better you will do in love. The more your assets even out, the more apt you are to make someone fall in love with you. Equity theorists tell us the more equitable a romantic relationship is, the more likely it is to progress to marriage.[37]

 What Currency 'Buys' a Good Partner?

Proponents of the equity principle list six elements which are assets on the 'open market' when lovers go husband or wife shopping:

1. Physical appearance
2. Possessions or money
3. Status or prestige
4. Information or knowledge
5. Social graces or personality
6. Inner nature

Researchers tell us that, in the happiest relationships, the partners are more or less equal in each of the above categories. If not, their qualities balance each other out across the board.

As an example, let us take category number one, physical appearance. Studies all over the world (the United States, Canada, Germany, Japan) show that men and women usually wind up marrying people who are just about as attractive as they are. A group of psychologists observed young couples at social events and rated their appearance on a scale similar to the now-legendary 1–10 rating scale popularized by the film *10*.[38] They found that 60 per cent of the couples were separated by only one point on the scale, and 85 per cent were separated by two points or less.

I decided to put these findings to my own informal test. For several weeks, everywhere I went – to the cinema, shopping, to parties, to restaurants – I watched husbands and wives, boyfriends and girlfriends. On a scale of one to ten, I rated their appearance. Never were they more than two points apart! Try it.

Researchers tell us if a couple is not equal in the *same* category, usually their assets across the list even out. For example, how often, walking down the street, have you passed a stunning woman on the arm of a pinch-faced, much-older man? What was your first thought? Admit it, you probably said to yourself, 'Gosh, he must be really rich.' You see a handsome man walking with his arm around a very plain woman and you muse, 'Gosh, she must have a great personality.' That is the equity, or horse-trading, principle at work. It cannot be denied. Good looks, lots of money, and high social status are definitely legal tender in the acquisition of love.

Back in the 1930s several Oakland, California, educators observed fifth- and sixth-grade girls cavorting on the playground. They rated the little girls according to their looks. About twenty years later, a sociologist got hold of the results of the old study and tracked down the young women to find out what kinds of husbands they had married. The researcher found that the prettier the girl, the 'better' she had done in securing a mate. The more attractive girls had richer and more powerful husbands. The less attractive girls had not done so well.

Does this mean our face is our fortune? Well, with minor changes we must go through life with the same mug. Fortunately, that is not the only currency with which we buy love. A pleasant personality, courteous social graces, and knowledge or information that your partner can benefit from also give you points.

Throughout this book you can find techniques to magnify the qualities that make your Quarry fall in love with you. In the cases of those attributes that can't be genuinely greatly enhanced (such as your looks, your money, and your prestige), I offer you techniques to enhance his or her *perception* of them. Before exploring methods to manipulate perceptions, however, let's get a reality check on how beautiful, how rich, or how powerful you really want your partner to be if your goal is, as I assume, to find happiness in love.

Here is a surprising truth – all the studies support it. Your chances of finding and keeping true love are even better if you don't marry someone drop-dead gorgeous, filthy rich, or a prince or princess. Why? *Because balanced benefits make happy campers*, especially in the long run. People are happier when their assets equal out. Let's peel back a few layers on the equity principle and get a reality check on how much you want to manipulate it. Then, if you still do, I will show you how.

Chapter Twenty Five

How Can I Use the Equity Principle to Find Love?

 You Really Don't Want to Marry the Handsome Prince or the Beautiful Princess

Practically every young American girl of my generation tucked the covers daintily around herself every night dreaming of the handsome prince who was someday going to come riding by on his white horse. He would, of course, fall madly in love with her and scoop her up, and they would live happily ever after.

The prince didn't always have to be a handsome Prince. He could be a rich Prince, a wonderfully kind Prince, or a strong and sensitive Prince. Perhaps, we dreamed, our prince would be a poet, or an artist, or maybe a famous actor Prince. As we grew older, our dream did not change. We simply expanded the definition of *prince*. He could be an internationally esteemed doctor, a brilliant CEO, a Silicon Valley sage, or a politician. But, whatever role we cast him in, he was the prince.

Huntresses, maybe even now you still believe that someday your prince will come. Well, guess what? He may come. But, when you see the results of the studies on love, you will realize *you don't want him to come*! Women, if it is happiness you seek, you don't want to marry the handsome prince. Men, you don't want to marry the beautiful princess.

Sour grapes? Not at all. Unless you were born in a royal crib – unless you are equally beautiful, equally rich, equally accomplished – life with a prince or princess would be inequitable. Therefore, you would be miserable.

'No,' you may protest. 'If I married someone better looking, richer, more accomplished – for simplicity let's just say *better* – if I married someone better than me, I'd be thrilled.' Yes, the studies tell us, but not for long. The equity theory proves you would soon be unhappy. The more superior your partner is to you, the quicker you would both feel wretched. When there is an imbalance in a relationship, both partners sense the inequity and try to restore balance. In other words, they try to even the score.

 ## 'Why Don't I Want to Get Married?'

It is easy to understand why, in an inequitable relationship, the superior partner might be dissatisfied. After the first blush of love wears off, he or she looks around and feels deserving of a much better deal. But what about the inferior partner? Shouldn't he or she feel darn lucky to have bagged such a great mate? Supposedly, yes, but in reality, the inferior partner will wind up worried, insecure, and always afraid of not measuring up.

This is true not only in marriages. Researchers interviewed 500 dating couples at the University of Wisconsin to determine whether their partners brought more, less, or equal assets to the relationship.[39] The more equitable the partner's assets, the happier the couples were. If one of the partners was much richer or more attractive, there was an imbalance, and discontent soon set in.

Insidious things start happening and the inequality monster starts eating away the love. In inequitable marriages, partners start taking advantage of the relationship to even the score. The 'superior' partner might start to make subtle demands, like feeling entitled to conversation whenever he or she wants it, or solitude whenever the mood strikes. A superior wife might get lazy with verbal expressions of love and affection or withhold sex. If she is already giving more than her husband, she figures subconsciously, 'Why should I work harder to make his sex life fulfilling?' A superior husband might even feel justified embarking on an extramarital affair. After all, he tells himself, 'I deserve more.'

The poor inferior in the relationship is doomed to living a life of insecurity about their love or having to 'swallow it' whenever the partner decides to take advantage of the relationship. The happiness at having bagged such a great mate soon turns into the day-to-day reality of always being number two. It is no fun being number two and spending your life trying harder.

Princess Di and Charles certainly did their bit to destroy the myth of the joy of marrying the prince. And in Hollywood, where one's market value changes daily like the NASDAQ, divorce is practically as common as marriage.

Let's say you are a princess with lots of money and good looks. You fall in love with the handsome, sensitive plumber who comes to fix the pipes on Daddy's yacht. Because you believe in true love, you marry him. Now, obviously you call the shots in the relationship, like choosing where to holiday and what kind of car to buy. At first you both consider it fair for you to make the decision because, after all, Daddy's money is paying for it.

But Sensitive Plumber has pride. As time goes by, his ego cannot take it. Even though he felt lucky when he married you, the love affair ends in bitter divorce. You really did not do anything wrong. He didn't, either. He is a nice guy, You played fair. It's just that the *inequity* overwhelmed the two of you. He winds up much happier with the waitress from the coffee shop.

'What Happens if Inequity Strikes After We're Married?'

Sometimes couples start out balanced, and inequity strikes *after* the marriage. If one of the partners, through no fault of his or her own, slips even a few notches, problems can arise.

I have a friend Laura, a television reporter, who was thrilled when she found the man of her dreams. He was a kind and intelligent gentleman who happened to be a big maker and shaker in international business. They married, and Laura was happy giving up her New York job and moving to California with him. About once a year, Laura visited me in New York. Every evening Bob would call. She always sounded so loving and deferential to him on the phone.

Two years ago, through a series of bad deals, Bob lost practically all his money. Laura still visits me (when they can afford the airfare). Bob still calls. But, sadly, I hear a different tone in her voice. Now she sounds snippy and domineering when she talks to him. Laura is starting to bemoan the great job she gave up when she married Bob, and she is now looking into television opportunities in New York. She says transferring back would be no problem. I don't place any bets on Laura and Bob being together same time next year.

I have another friend, Sally, whom I met in college. Everyone liked Sally because she was what we used to call the archetypical dizzy blonde. Sally was not impressively bright, but she was strikingly beautiful. She married a sportive and very accomplished man named Jim. Sally was blissful in her marriage until recently, when she gained a lot of weight. Sally complains, 'I can't understand it. Jim treats me so differently now. He's not running round, but he's moody. He doesn't do as many chores around the house. He doesn't talk to me anymore. Our sex life is sagging, and it's as though he's just not sensitive to my feelings.'

This would not surprise proponents of the equity principle. They would say Jim is subconsciously restoring the balance.

Researchers analysing their changing relationship would say, 'When Sally and Jim got married, she brought physical beauty to the relationship. He brought a good nature. These are tangible assets. If her beauty wanes, so does the asset he brought to the table.' Jim is certainly not kicking Sally out. He still loves her, of course. Subconsciously Jim is simply balancing the score by letting down on some of his pleasing habits.

Inequity can also occur when one of the partners makes a mistake. If one is caught in an extramarital affair, the other might go into a well of frosty silence and stay in that funk until the partner who messed up commits enough loving acts to make up for it. That can take years.

Studies cite dramatic examples of one partner's coming into a huge inheritance or, conversely losing his or her job or even being tragically disfigured in an accident. That destroys the balance of the relationship.

The subjects in these studies were not mean, heartless people who left their partners. They simply subconsciously evened the score in a myriad of small ways such as withholding expressions of affection, letting down on their physical appearance, or becoming reluctant to make self-sacrifices for their partner's benefit. The superior partner might refuse to do chores, take a stronger stand on which parents to visit for the holidays, or suggest separate vacations. Small reactions lead to big misery in relationships that become unequal.

Hunters, Huntresses, if after all these warnings about how you don't want to get married, you are still thinking, 'Well, maybe finding a partner just a *little* higher on that vulgar inventory of assets would be OK,' come with me. You cannot really change your looks, your bank account, or your breeding to match the Quarry you want to bag, but you can change their opinion of your assets. Let's start with the one that's the toughest to manipulate. It is number one on the love assets list: physical appearance.

Chapter Twenty Six

How Important Are Looks?

How important are looks? Let me put it this way. After doing initial research for this chapter, it was a tough choice between plastic surgery or suicide. First, let's get the bad news out of the way for those of us, male or female, who are less than a 10 in the looks department. *Looks count*!

Remember in secondary school when you asked about a blind date's looks and your best friend said, 'Oh, she's got a great personality' or 'He's a really nice guy.' The kiss of death, right? Yes, looks count on first meeting, especially to men. However, looks are a *perception*, and we can manipulate perceptions. What God cheated us out of in the looks department, we can make up for through clever techniques that have a lot more to do with your Quarry's first impressions of you (your body language, self-image, and communication skills) than they do with make-up.

What do we consider good-looking? It varies, of course, from culture to culture. In our country, thin is in. (Not so for the Sirono women from Bolivia who constantly gorge themselves to become a nice fat armful for their men.) American men prefer to kiss slightly curved Cupid's-bow lips. (Not so for Ubangis, who put saucers in their lips to stretch them out like pancakes.)

Different standards of beauty prevail around the world, but one thing remains constant. Mother Nature plays a role in telling us who is hot and who is not. Even in modern-day America, women like a man with strong features who looks like he would be a good, caring provider. Men like a woman who looks like she is sexy and could bear healthy children. Studies tell us precisely what is in vogue.

 ## What Types of Looks Do Women Like?

Here is what a group of researchers found that women most liked in a man's face:

> Women are attracted to men whose appearances elicit their nurturant feelings; who appear to possess sexual maturity and dominance characteristics; who seem sociable, approachable and of high social status ...
>
> Individuals who display an optimal combination of neotenous (boyish) features of large eyes, the mature features of prominent cheekbones and a large chin, the expressive feature of a big smile, and high-status clothing were seen more attractive than other men.[40]

What type of body do women like? American women generally prefer men of average build, but bigger above the waist than below. The studies tell us they prefer V's to pears.[41] However, taste varies depending on the class of the woman judging the male anatomy. Women on the lower end of the socio-economic totem pole prefer muscle men. Conversely, highly paid professional women find hefty beefcake downright distasteful. They go for the dark, slim, and sensitive body types.

What about height? One assumes the taller the better because our culture venerates height. In fact, practically every president elected in the United States since 1900 was the taller of the two candidates. The *Wall Street Journal* reported that taller graduating college students (6´2˝ and over) received an average starting salary 12.4 per cent higher than those who were under six feet tall. Yet, in the sexual arena, apparently taller is not better. Women of all sizes – short, medium, and tall – rated a variety of men equal in all features except height. The medium sizers won.

Gentlemen, speaking of size (yes, the size of *it*), the only source I can turn to is a recent article in a popular woman's magazine called 'Is Big Really Better?' The article equivocated (lest readers' husbands get hold of the article and be emotionally destroyed). However, a photograph accompanying the article left the question open. Two attractive women were shown rolling on the floor in hysterics as one of their friends held up a baby finger.

 ## What Types of Looks Do Men Like?

When answering researchers' questions about women's looks, men were less articulate. A typical answer was, 'Uh, erm, well, you know [grunt, grunt], uh, good-looking.' However, a group of resolute scientists plodded on and zeroed in on what the average male considers attractive.

Yes, thin is definitely in. For women especially. In an analysis of singles' ads, researchers discovered, out of twenty-eight desirable qualities, thinness topped the list for men.[42] Again, this varied with the class and personality of the man. More extroverted and lower-class men choose large-breasted, wide-hipped women. More introverted and upper-class males choose smaller-framed women.

A group of men from various classes was shown photos of large-breasted nudes in typical pin-up poses along with some pictures of more fully clothed attractive women. The results were as expected when the men were asked which they would like for a roll in the hay. However, when questioned on which they would prefer as a wife, both upper- and lower-class men chose the more clothed woman. Many of the upper-class men even preferred the clothed lady for a roll in the hay (or a tryst in the backseat of their Mercedes).

Unfortunately, the studies were not any more enlightening on the specific facial features men like. This is probably because, like in all other aspects of their lives, men don't pay as much attention to detail as women do.

There was a time when our culture was obsessed with symmetry. No longer. And, in times gone by, men wanted women in the lighter ranges of their own ethnic colouring. Women preferred just the opposite. Darker-hued men got top points. However, as our melting pot boils faster, the old blonde-haired, blue-eyed, angel-faced beauty standard is rapidly changing. Some of today's top beauties are very different from that stereotypical idea. Now it's *the look*. Fortunately, if you weren't born with *the look*, you can get it – with a little brains, some imagination, and a make-up bag.

The only generalization we can make on looks is that both sexes prefer people with clear complexions, a slender body, shiny hair, straight white teeth, and clear eyes – in other words, healthy.

'How Can I Make My Quarry Think I'm Better Looking?'

Beauty is not an objective entity. Like the proverbial sound in the forest which must be heard to be a sound, beauty has to be beheld by someone to be beauty. Beauty is a perception, a judgment call. Hairstyle, clothing, and make-up aside (I leave that to other books), here is how you can manipulate your Quarry's perception of your looks.

While I was researching physical appearance, a friend sent me a videotape of a segment of the American television show *20/20* aired some time ago on physical attractiveness. In one sequence, a strikingly beautiful blonde (an actress) stood on the side of the road by her supposedly stranded car. Passing cars and trucks came screeching to a halt. Men risked life and limb galloping across four lanes to help the lovely damsel in distress. Several men fought over which lucky man was going to go get her petrol for her.

In the next segment, another actress stood by the side of the highway. Same clothes. Same stranded car. However, this woman was less attractive, or so judged the programme's producers. Did cars come to a screeching halt to help her? Did men gallop across four lanes to help her? No. The cars went whizzing by. One or two slowed down but, after the drivers checked her out, they sped away. One car stopped, but the male driver simply pointed to where she could go to get some petrol herself.

Afterward, the programme's hosts interviewed the two actresses seated side by side. I pushed the pause button on my VCR to get a closer look at the two women. I scrutinized one, then the other, then the first again. I thought, 'There's not that much difference in their looks!' But, being female, I presumed that perhaps I'm no judge, so I decided to get a male opinion. I showed the frozen frame to a male friend. He agreed. 'Not so much difference.'

What was it? I played the entire sequence for my friend. 'Oh, sure,' he announced. *Now* he could see it. 'Yes, the first actress is definitely prettier.'

It took a third viewing for me to unravel the mystery. The first actress smiled at passing cars. She cocked her head, threw her shoulders back, and pushed her breasts out. She looked happy, fun-loving, sure of herself – therefore beautiful. The second actress just leaned against her car with a dejected expression on her face. She made no eye contact with passing traffic. She looked miserable and crossed her arms in front of her chest, hiding two of her very good assets. She looked unhappy, grumpy, unsure of herself – therefore homely. Beautiful women *move* differently than their plainer sisters do.

This leads us to a technique to change your Quarry's perception of your looks. Develop confident and beautiful body language. You will actually appear more beautiful when you move with grace and enthusiasm. Beauty is as beauty moves.

TECHNIQUE 47 (FOR HUNTRESSES):

Move Like a 10

Can you fool Mother Nature? No. But you *can* fool a man.
Convince yourself that you are the most beautiful creature that ever graced the planet. Then *move* accordingly.

Men, does a similar technique work for you? Yes. Your physical movements definitely affect how alluring you are to women.

Recently, after one of my seminars, a man asked me for some advice on approaching women. He was a good-looking fellow, but he stood slumped in front of me, his arms dangling like he had no further use for them. His eyes periodically darted away from mine in shyness. He asked me what opening lines work with a woman. I wanted to shake him and say, 'Hey, forget what comes out of your mouth! First shape up your body language.' Women are attracted to men who move in a strong, self-assured, and masculine fashion.

TECHNIQUE 48 (FOR HUNTERS):

Move Like a Hunk

Men, make strong, smooth, bold movements. Walk strong. Look like you know where you are going and why.
Take the woman's arm when crossing the street, help her in and out of cars, and make other manly gestures that women find so seductive.

Countless studies conducted on how your physical appearance affects your success in love lead us to the following unusual technique. It will definitely increase your chances of finding your special someone.

 ## How to Beef Up Your Odds on Making the Kill

If I told you that, by heeding the results of the studies, you could more than double your chance of success the next time you try to pick up a PLP, would you believe it? Believe it!

In singles' clubs everywhere, Hunters are getting shot down when they try to pick up a lady. Every night Huntresses go home alone feeling like white rabbits glancing at their biological clocks. Marriage-minded men and women everywhere are griping that they will always be supporting cast at the wedding rather than the stars. Why is this happening? Most singles are barking up the wrong trees, howling after impossible prey. These lone wolves might as well be baying at the moon.

How can you better your odds? First, go after more equal targets in the physical appearance department. Men, it is rough for you to keep your eyeballs off the best-looking women on the premises. You want the most attractive date possible, but aren't you tired of getting your ego bruised every time you say hello? Women, it is easier for you to go after men within your own attractiveness range because women usually are more appreciative of inner qualities.

Start by taking a good look at yourself in the mirror. (Go ahead, you can cheat. Get all dressed up first.) Eyeball yourself objectively. Rate yourself on the *10* scale. (If you need some help, ask your closest friend.) Are you a four, a six, an eight, better? Now, with that number in mind, look at the Quarry you are trying to score with. Rate him or her on the same scale. If your Quarry is one or two points within your range, go for it. If not, forget it. The studies show you are wasting your time.

Do you enjoy kisses and cuddles? The psychologists also predicted that couples similar in attractiveness would be more affectionate. They observed couples at parties and singles' gathering spots. And they guessed right. Whether the couple was two 'beauties' or two 'uglies', they seemed happier and played footsie a lot more if they were of similar attractiveness. A full 60 per cent of the similar couples nuzzled each other, 46 per cent of the moderately similar couples caressed, and only 22 per cent of the less similar couples ever touched each other.

It seems that birds of a feather flock together – at least when it comes to plumage.

TECHNIQUE 49

Mirror, Mirror, on the Wall

To dramatically increase your chances of success with new Quarry, only pursue prey within one or two points' difference on the attractiveness scale. This technique also ups the odds on lifetime happiness with your partner.

Now it is time to move on to the next two commodities on the equity scale: possessions (or money) and status (or prestige).

Chapter Twenty Seven

Pursuing Rich and Famous Prey

While writing this book, I excitedly told anyone who would listen that I was exploring what science says makes people fall in love. If my listeners were single and searching, I would then ask them what type of partner they would like to make fall in love with them. Sometimes, after the first wave of predictable answers like someone kind, loving, and intelligent, came another swell. Some love-seekers gushed about finding a lover who was rich, powerful, cultured, and even high-class.

It is with a degree of embarrassment that I write this sensitive chapter, but the market dictates. If you have set your sights on Quarry way above your own status, you need special trappings. In other parts of the book there are techniques to come across as more attractive, intelligent, gracious, and kind. Now let's talk about how to come across as richer, more refined, higher class, or higher status to attract like Quarry.

The Look of Money

What special hunting outfit do you need to pursue pedigreed prey? Obviously, you are going to leave your Hawaiian shirt and polyester tracksuit in the closet. Rich birds have a special eagle eye for those of the same expensive feathers. The look of wealth goes from your haircut right down to your feet. Don't try to sneak one cheap detail into your ensemble. Spring for a fifty-dollar haircut, an expensive watch, real gold jewellery. It shows.

A pair of cheap shoes stands out like a sign flashing imposter in otherwise million-dollar duds. Better to sport twenty-dollar socks fraying at the ankle than new cheapies you picked up in the supermarket checkout line.

TECHNIQUE 50

Let Your Rags Show Riches

Gentlemen, go for one handmade suit. Make sure your tailor is expert in the delightfully arcane details of flaps, vents, lapels, and stitching.

Ladies, you can dress off the rack, but make sure the rack has a recognizable designer's name over it.

When chasing costly Quarry, make sure nothing adorns your body that costs less than £75, with the possible exceptions of your socks and undies.

 ## The Sound of Class

Another obvious class determinant is language. Talking rich does not mean flinging out fakeries like, 'When my chauffeur drove me to Elizabeth Arden this morning in my Bentley ...' It *does* mean paying attention to the words you drop. Avoid low-class klunkers.

Using euphemisms for certain words reveals lower stature. In 1956, Nancy Mitford wrote a magazine article about upper-class and non-upper-class language, or *U* (for upper-class) and *Non-U* (for non-upper-class, or lower-class) language.[43]

As soon as the magazine hit the news stands, it caused a national frenzy. As Phillip Toynbee put it in the *Observer*, the article became a sort of a 'How to Tell Your Friends from the Apes'. Mitford gave examples of U and Non-U words. For example, a very proper upper-class Brit, upon being introduced, would say, 'How do you do?' The other very upper-class Brit would nonsensically repeat the question back: 'How do you do?' However, a lower-class, or Non-U Brit, upon being asked, 'How do you do?' would actually have the crassness to answer the question: 'Very well, thank you,' or, worse, 'Pleased to meet you, I'm sure.'

Another big giveaway of apelike status is using euphemisms. Lower classes used words like *wealthy*, whereas the upper classes called it like it is, *rich*. The Non-U crowd euphemized *lavatory paper*, whereas upper-class people said *toilet paper*.

When pursuing pedigreed prey, simply stamp out euphemisms. Call a spade a spade. It's *toilet*, not *little boy's room*. It's *penis* and *vagina*, not *pecker* and *pussy*. When they talk about their family jewels, they are referring to the ones in the safe on the wall. If a word is just too crude, resort to French. *Backside* is out. *Derrière* is in.

TECHNIQUE 51

Let Your Tongue Show Riches

To trap pedigreed prey, you needn't collect upper-class words and memorize them, but do cut out the euphemisms. (Don't forget to use the *Echoing* technique. It will save you from making many faux pas.)

When socializing with the upper class, pay attention to your speaking voice. Keep it low, keep it dulcet, and keep it *clear*. I once decided to give my voice a much needed boost and consulted an actress friend of mine, Barbara, who had a beautiful speaking voice. Barbara's voice had an elegant ring to it. In fact, she made a living doing voice-overs for expensive cars and jewellery.

I knew Barbara had invested several thousand dollars in voice training, so I asked her what she got out of it. Was it worth it?

'Yes,' she replied. 'But it could have all been summed up in one sentence.' In a voice dripping with rubies, Barbara told me to pronounce every syllable of every word.

TECHNIQUE 52

The Sound of Class

The secret to a well-heeled tongue is, quite simply, to pronounce all of your syllables and finish every word that issues forth from your mouth.

What Does the U Crowd Talk About?

If you intend to do much prospecting on Easy Street, learn the street language of the residents. Listen attentively to get the drift of conversations. You will soon sense that some topics are in, others are out. For example, the arts are in. How much something costs is out. (After all, the rich can have whatever they want, whenever they want it, and to heck with the cost.) Current events are in. Strong political opinions are out. Tributes are in. Teasing is out. Avocations are in. Vocations are out.

On rare occasions, I get invited (as the token working-class person, I am sure) to parties studded with people whose main battle in life is fighting off charities seeking donations. At most parties, I enjoy talking about my work, but at these gatherings, I have learned not to don a friendly smile and ask 'What do you do?' Many pedigreed pups don't *do* anything – at least not for pay.

In the case of prestigious prey? Well, you should just *know* what they do. It is an insult to ask.

TECHNIQUE 53

Don't Ask 'What Do You Do?'

Develop an ear for appropriate topics of conversation. Pedigreed and other prestigious prey have very sensitive toes. You don't want to go around stamping on them.

Above all, avoid the favourite party question, 'And, what do you do?' It tags you as *so* working class.

Use Status Words with Status Prey

People from richer backgrounds have richer clothes, richer houses, richer cars, and richer vocabularies. They don't necessarily have big cars, but they do tend to avoid the common little ones. It is the same with their words. They don't often use big ones, but they do avoid the common little ones that have little impact.

To be well-spoken in the well-heeled, high-accomplishment crowd, use the technique I call *your personal thesaurus*. Think of some words you often use, for example, the overused words *good* and *smart*. It is very common to say, 'You look good' or 'That's a smart idea.'

Take a thesaurus (a dictionary of synonyms) down from the library shelf. Look up *smart* and *good*. You will find dozens of richer synonyms. Like trying on a suit of clothes, choose three or four words that seem to fit your personality. Then, Hunters, the next time you want to compliment your class Quarry and tell her she looks good, say, 'Oh, Sue, you look *ravishing*,' or *stunning*. Or 'Sue, how *striking* you look,' or 'Oh, my goodness, you look *elegant*.'

Huntresses, you would like to compliment your highbrow Quarry by telling him he did something smart? Instead, say, 'Oh, George, that was so *clever* of you', or how *resourceful*, or *ingenious*. 'George, that was so *astute* of you.'

Give high rollers high-rolling compliments. Cultivate your own personal thesaurus of not big words, but words you like, elegant words that fit you. Use them a few times with your friends and family. Soon, just like breaking in a new pair of shoes, you will be comfortable chatting with your well-spoken Quarry.

♥

TECHNIQUE 54

Your Personal Thesaurus

To convey a rich background, choose rich words from the thesaurus. Like a beautiful necklace, try them on, then let them fall, like pearls, from your lips while chatting with your prestigious prey.

♥

Chapter Twenty Eight

Upping Your Ante in Other Assets

 Knowledge, Social Graces, and Inner Beauty Are Tangible Assets

So far, we have talked about increasing your market value through manipulating your Quarry's impression of your physical appearance, possessions or money, and status or prestige. These are but the first three assets that equity principle scientists say influence love. They are important but, by no means, the most important. In fact, many people prefer the next three qualities by far. They are information or knowledge, social graces or personality, and inner nature.

Let's talk about information, or knowledge. The pursuit of knowledge is a lifetime commitment, one that brings you deep joy throughout your life. Intelligence gained through knowledge can also be a potent asset in making someone fall in love with you.

Many women, myself included, find the seedy, professorial, pipe-smoking, suede-patches-on-the-elbows-of-his-sweater type of man very attractive. I once flipped over a man whom other women might call a poor, homely recluse because he was a genius on the computer. His knowledge deeply impressed me, and I wanted to learn from him. Hunters, especially in today's world, women have a tendency to fall in love with men who can help them professionally. Your knowledge is an aphrodisiac to bright, ambitious women.

Social graces, or personality, is the fifth asset which gives you a higher value on the open love market. Techniques throughout this book are offered to help you deal with these two aspects. Heed them all.

The final asset on the list, but by no means the least, is your inner nature. Perhaps this is the most important of all – it certainly is the deepest. To make someone fall in love with you, strive always to have loving thoughts about them and about others. Give selflessly to other persons when there is no reward in sight. Be sexually faithful, financially responsible, and personally flexible. The list of inner nature qualities goes on. You probably never thought of them in these terms, but they are all marketable assets you bring to a relationship. Everything you learn, every experience you process, every fine quality you develop, is a tangible benefit in making someone fall in love with you.

TECHNIQUE 55

Up Your Ante in Intangibles

To up your market value, never stop learning, never stop developing your personality and social skills, and always strive to develop fine inner qualities. They are as good as golden bullets to pierce your Quarry's heart.

Chapter Twenty Nine

Help Them Convince Themselves That They Love You

 Let Your Quarry Do Favours for You

Loving someone, and being loved by this person, is a convoluted pattern of reward and punishment. We are happy when the person we love gives us gifts or does favours for us, and we receive equally as much joy doing the same for our beloved. But, according to the equity principle of love, somewhere buried in our subconscious is the *scorecard*. Who is doing more for whom, and does it all balance out?

It doesn't have to be tit for tat in equal actions. The tit can be the joy we receive for doing tat. For example, Huntresses, if you love a man, you actually *enjoy* driving him to work when his car breaks down. His appreciation is your reward. Hunters, you *enjoy* giving her flowers. Her smile is your reward. Are we forced to drive him to work or to give her flowers? No. We do it because we *want* to.

Why do we want to? The answer is obvious. We do it because we love him, because we love her. Or so we tell ourselves.

This leads us into an intriguing aspect of the love game. You can use it to make people convince themselves that they are in love with you. Researchers call it the *cognitive-consistency theory*. Cognitive consistency says that individuals strive to keep their cognitions psychologically consistent and that, when inconsistencies arise, they strive to restore consistency. In other words, people strive to keep their actions in tune with their convictions. Whenever they do something, they want to feel they are doing it for a good reason, because they want to do it.

Often individuals who volunteer for a worthy cause value the task more if they are not offered money. Studies have shown that the harder a person works for a volunteer group, the more he or she values the organization's efforts. If offered financial compensation, most people would see the task more as a job they *had* to do.

People watch their own actions and then instinctively adjust their philosophy and feelings to match. They say to themselves, 'Golly, I'm working so hard for this group. I must really believe in their goals.' That way they achieve cognitive consistency. If they continued working hard and did not believe in the goals, they would have to admit to themselves that they are stupid or screwed up, and nobody wants to do that. It is the same in love.

> If you find yourself doing for someone things that, in themselves, are not rewarding, you are likely to come to the conclusion that you must like that person, because you could not be doing the things for their own sake ... thus you achieve cognitive consistency.[44]

People don't only observe other people. They observe themselves. A great part of our self-perception and what we believe we feel comes from watching our own actions.[45] Thus, if we do something for another person that is in itself unrewarding, our self-talk tells us it means we really love them.

If you get up early to drive your Quarry around or find yourself giving her gifts, you must be doing it because you are in love. Why else would you put yourself out or spend your hard-earned money? This translates into the following technique to boost your Quarry's perception that he or she is in love with you.

TECHNIQUE 56

Let Him or Her Do Favours for You

Let your Quarry do little favours for you and give you gifts. Thank him or her, but don't appear *too* grateful. Act as though it is perfectly logical for your Quarry to be putting himself or herself out for you.

To restore *cognitive consistency*, your Quarry will be convinced that he or she must really love you.

A word of warning: don't go overboard with this one. If you do, it could tip the delicate balance. If your Quarry feels he or she is doing *too* much, the relationship could capsize and sink.

Hey! What About 'O Lyric Love, Half Angel and Half Bird'?

'Where,' you might well ask, 'does the purity, the beauty, and the selfless kind of love come in? What about couples who pledge eternal love, till death do us part – and mean it?'

We can, of course, achieve that beautiful love – in time. Actually, the lyric love Robert Burns wrote about and the fundamentally practical, egocentric discoveries scientists have made about love are not totally incompatible. Many couples stay together, stay happy, and stay in love for a lifetime, but if you look above their heads, you will see the great scorecard in the sky. There is probably a balance in what each partner brings to the relationship.

Often there are subjective values that outsiders cannot see. At any isolated point in time, the relationship can appear inequitable to strangers. When partners commit to a lifetime relationship, it is no longer tit for tat on a daily, weekly, or even monthly basis. The scorecard *can* become unequal for a while. For instance, a wife may support her husband while he goes through medical school. She is in the superior position for a few years, and he is getting the better deal. Then, when he has his degree, he is expected to either finance her education or support the family in style to even the score.

What about relationships that seem very one-sided for a long time, such as a loving husband or wife who selflessly cares for an ailing partner in their later years? Well, years spent together actually become one of the assets brought to the relationship. You might not think of it in those terms, but the care-giving partner is paying back the beloved spouse for the years of happiness received in the relationship.

Once two people who love each other have made a commitment, the boat can stay afloat even if it tilts in one direction. But it must rock back the other way before they reach the ultimate balance and can hope for a smooth journey. A person can accept favours for a while from a partner, but the truly wise ones pay back to keep the balance of assets in the relationship on a par.

Why have I placed such emphasis on exploring this philosophy? Upon this rock-solid foundation, equity, we build many of the techniques to make someone fall in love with you. In fact, all of the techniques in this book are designed to boost your value in love relationships to make your Potential Love Partner fall harder, faster.

Part Five

Early-Date

Gender-Menders

Is There Love After Eden?

Chapter Thirty

'I Hope He or She's Not an Idiot Like All the Others'

Did you see the 1977 movie *Annie Hall?* When Diane Keaton is out with Woody Allen for the first time, a little bubble comes out of her head, saying, 'I hope he's not a jerk like all the others.' During the first moments of meeting you, your Quarry is hoping the same about you.

Early love is a delicate little flower. Its tiny petals are often crushed when one of the partners unknowingly commits a small blooper on the first date and turns the other off. A stupid joke, the slurping of a Coke, an unintended insult, all can abort the take-off and leave a new relationship burning on the side of the runway. Later in the love affair the same blooper might amount to no more than a slightly uncomfortable air pocket.

The fumbles we will explore here are gender-specific, and many are new unacceptables. With the emerging equality of men and women, actions that used to be taken for granted now drive the opposite sex bonkers. In another era, another society, another economy, a man could get away with spending every Friday night with the boys or whipping out a cigar at the table. His lady was expected to smile pleasantly as the smoke asphyxiated her. There was a time when a woman was expected to have no aspirations outside the home and to be interested only in 'woman-talk'. Men felt self-righteous leaving the women to 'prattle' as they retired into the den to deliberate on really important issues, like which cigar had the best flavour.

Times have changed. What used to be a resigned, 'Well, boys will be boys!' or 'Isn't that just like a woman?' is now grounds for your Quarry to depart for greener pastures. Today, Huntresses demand a sensitive man who will share their feelings. And Hunters envision a superwoman who gives them great company, great kids, great compassion, and great orgasms.

Does this new breed of sensitive man and superwoman exist? The question is academic, because it is not reality but your Quarry's *perceptions* we are dealing with. This section gives you techniques to convince your Quarry that you are indeed that extraordinary individual. You are a sensitive man. You are a superwoman.

Hunters, when you use some of the words and ideas I am going to suggest, your Quarry will say to herself, 'At last, a sensitive man – one who understands me and I can talk to.' Huntresses, when your Quarry hears some of the following words and sentiments coming from your feminine lips, he will say, 'At last, a sensible woman – one who understands me and I can relate to. This woman is really special. I think I'm in love.'

This section is especially valuable for capturing the heart of a gun-shy Quarry who, because he or she is fearful of relationships, often runs at the first sign of stereotypical gender behaviour. We will talk about the most common gender-specific fatal fumbles which usually appear on first dates and eat away at early love. I will show you how to avoid these pitfalls or at least not get thrown out of the game on a stupid penalty.

♥ 'I Want a Man I Can Talk to, a Woman Who Thinks Like a Man'

We spot the gender gap very early, in nursery schools and kindergartens everywhere. In the middle of the room, little boys are bashing other little boys. Meanwhile, around the nursery, little girls are sharing toys and holding deep communion with other little girls.

Unfortunately, the same gap splits many middle-class parties of marrieds right down the middle. The men stand centre stage arguing sports or politics, and the women, seated around the room, are supportively chatting with each other. Why the division? It is simply because men enjoy talking about certain subjects and women fancy others. Additionally, men have different styles of talking to women.

How can we translate this cleft into a technique to capture your Quarry? Learn how to captivate the opposite sex with your conversation. Discover what subjects interest him or her.

Hunters, to help a woman fall in love with you, look like a man, work like a man, walk like a man, talk deep-voiced like a man – but *be sensitive* like a woman. Intelligently discuss subjects which interest her. Huntresses, to help a man fall in love with you, look like a woman, smile like a woman, smell like a woman, speak softly like a woman – but *think* like a man. Intelligently discuss subjects that interest him.

Men, don't be frightened that you will sound effeminate discussing the subtleties women excel at, such as insights into people and their feelings. Being a fascinating conversationalist to a woman definitely does not detract from your masculinity. It merely makes you multidimensional and engrossing to talk to. Women, don't be concerned that discussing subjects the boys like makes you sound like one of the boys. Hearing subjects and sentiments close to a man's heart coming from your softly rounded feminine lips makes you a fascinating woman. He will think you are different from the rest of the females he has dated – a high compliment coming from a man.

How men and women differ in communication styles could, and has, filled volumes. I highly recommend you read a book dedicated to gender differences to give you a more in-depth understanding of men, women, and why they communicate so differently. Some excellent ones have been written by John Gray and Deborah Tannen, among others.

God revealed a cold and hard fact to us back in the Garden of Eden. Quite simply, He made men and women different. (One wonders if, in all His wisdom, He realized quite how different His creatures would turn out to be!)

John F. Kennedy said, 'If we cannot now end our differences, at least we can help make the world safe for diversity.' Let us alter one word of that sage advice.

Hunters, Huntresses, if we cannot now end our differences, at least we can help make the world safe for *love*. The following techniques are a good start.

Chapter Thirty One

What Is 'Man Talk' and What Is 'Woman Talk'? (Do They Exist?)

Decades of denial aside, men and women do enjoy discussing different subjects. All gender comments are generalizations, of course, but, usually, women are more people-centred and men are more thing-centred. Men enjoy talking about cars, gadgets, tools – about how something is made, how it works, how they can fix it, what its effect is, and how they control it. More intellectual men expand *things* to include ideas and concepts. But they still discuss how these concepts work, how they can fix them, how they affect the world, and how much power they have over them! Men exchange facts and opinions like trading cards. They like to play 'Who can trump whom?' with the cards. This competitive aspect of men's conversation is not advisable for a woman to emulate, but Huntresses, brushing up on sport, politics, cars, and computers increases your chances of communicating well with men. If you learn how to hold your own with some men by bantering about sabre saws and power drills, you will be a fascinating lady indeed.

When I was in high school, the literature on gender differences was limited to obscure studies, but my mother somehow intuitively knew about the cavernous conversational gap. The boys talked about cars, and the girls talked about boys. That left us girls at a conversational disadvantage on our dates. After a disastrously silent evening with a boy, I cried in my mother's lap. I told her I couldn't think of anything to talk about and had been frozen with shyness. My mother stroked my hair, dried my tears, and told me she would have a surprise for me the next day that would help. I believed in Mum and expected a miracle. Even if she had to fly a chunk of the Blarney Stone in from Ireland so I could kiss it and get the gift of gab, she would pull through for me.

TECHNIQUE 57 (FOR HUNTRESSES):

Brush Up on Man-Talk

Take a conversational cruise across the gender gap. Huntresses, become conversant in concepts, politics, objects, big toys, sports, and other male subjects.

Show him you are smart, but remember – not *too* smart.

Pull through she did. Better than the Blarney Stone, she bought me a book on cars – all the current models. I became something of an expert on the differences between Chevys, Fords, and Buicks. I could even discuss what went on under the bonnet. It got so I could keep up my end of the conversation when the subject turned (as it inevitably did) to carburettors, alternators, cam-shafts, and exhaust manifolds. Mum's book got my self-confidence with boys going. Huntresses, you may not find discussing cars, facts, sports, business, and politics as interesting as psychology, philosophy, relationships, reactions, and trends, but your Quarry will find you a more intriguing woman if you can hold your own while pitching phenomenons and numbers around with him.

A man in one of my seminars told me that the reason he asked his current girlfriend out was because, when they met, they had an engrossing discussion of whether slip-joint or round-nosed pliers would be better to have in a basic tool kit. He added, of course, that *he* won the argument. Huntresses, you want to be smart in male subjects. But not smarter than your Quarry. Does this sound like outdated fifties retro-pap advice? Of course it does, but it still holds. I learned this the hard way a long time ago.

On the evening of my high school prom, my date arrived on my doorstep. He pinned a corsage on my padded bust. I took his arm and we walked to his car. It wouldn't start. Thanks to Mum's book, I suspected the problem. I looked under his bonnet and made a silent analysis.

I then ran out into the street and flagged down a taxi. Not to take us to the dance, but to borrow the driver's jumper cables. Tottering in my first pair of high heels, I attached jumper cables to my date's dead battery and got his car engine purring. I knew he would be impressed.

He never called again.

I recently told this story to a male friend and, in a truly candid moment, he empathized with my poor humiliated date. Eventual equality aside, some things will never change.

TECHNIQUE 58 (FOR HUNTERS):

Brush Up on 'Woman-Talk'

Hunters, make your conversation more psychologically oriented. Converse with your Quarry in terms of people, feelings, philosophy, rationale, and intuition.

Hunters, here is a similar suggestion for you. Generally, women have excellent insights into people, their problems, and their responses to various situations. They often talk about health, the arts, personal growth, and sometimes spiritual subjects. When discussing their work, women are more apt to explore how individuals work together and what constitutes a smooth and supportive work environment, not who's on top and who's on bottom. Learn to thoughtfully probe feelings.

Gentlemen, pick up a copy of *Psychology Today*, a magazine with a readership of intelligent women. It is an excellent way to brush up on what subjects are hot for women.

These are generalizations, to be sure. There is always the man who enjoys discussing the deeper aspects of human relationships and the woman who enjoys a tough political argument. You will spot these rare birds, but they will be hard to catch. The insightful man will be in the company of beautiful women, and the clever woman will already be dating some heavy hitters.

Chapter Thirty Two
'How Do You *Feel* About That?'

Ever since they were little girls, women have shown spooky intuition when picking up on subtle tones of voice and facial expressions. The gentle sex is eerily expert at knowing how someone feels. A man, conversely, can't pick up on a sad face until his tie is drenched in his partner's tears.

Perhaps that is why women discuss feelings and men (because they are no good at it) seldom bring up the subject. Women, when talking with their friends, often ask each other how they feel about a certain situation. (The last time some men used the word *feel* was when they told their high school buddies they got to feel up a girl in the backseat.)

Hunter, you will distinguish yourself as a rare man indeed, if, while a woman is talking, you interject the elementary question, 'How do you *feel* about that?' You can ask the question about practically anything. Say she is talking about her home or something her sister did, her farther said, or her friend asked. Maybe she is telling you about her job, what her boss said, or what her co-worker did. No matter what she is discussing, she has feelings on the subject and, unlike you, she is probably more in touch with those feelings. She can articulate them better.

Here is a foolproof technique to make a woman perceive you as a truly sensitive man.

TECHNIQUE 59 (FOR HUNTERS):

'How Do You Feel About That?'

Hunters, *whatever* she is discussing, simply ask, 'How do you feel about that?' Go ahead, force yourself.

After she pulls her jaw back up to get it operable, she will respond enthusiastically.

Huntresses, can you ask a man how he feels about a particular situation? Sure, but early in a relationship, he will probably consider it an irrelevant female question. He might give you a one- or two-word answer which you, of course would interpret as abrupt. Things could spiral down from there. Men simply do not usually think first about their feelings, just as you are not as comfortable thinking in competitive terms.

Suppose, in conversation with a man, you tell him how, instead of one of your female co-workers, you got a promotion. The man suddenly asks, 'Good going. How did you *trump* her?' The question would take you aback. Your internal dialogue would probably say, 'Well, I didn't trump her. I simply was given the promotion because I deserved it.' You would, of course, answer him politely, but the competitive male nature of his question would not endear him to you.

Women tend to be less competitive. They enjoy winning, but no special sense of victory comes from the defeat of the loser. His asking 'How did you trump her?' is not a question women readily relate to. Likewise, 'How do you *feel* about' a certain situation is not a question a man can readily relate to. Unless you are talking with one of the rare men who enjoys exploring his feelings, play it safe. Save your feelings questions for later in the relationship – much later.

TECHNIQUE 60 (FOR HUNTRESSES):

Don't Explore 'Feelings' Too Early in a Relationship

Huntresses, until the relationship is in safe waters or you detect that your Quarry is the sensitive type, do not go overboard by asking a man how he feels about a situation. You may rock the boat before it gets launched.

Chapter Thirty Three
'Excuse Me, Could You Tell Me Where ...'

No exploration of the wondrous differences between Homo sapiens *m.* and Homo sapiens *f.* would be complete without addressing the former's (men's) hesitance to ask directions. One of the reasons, I am sure, that NASA decided to have female astronauts is so there would be somebody to ask directions when they got to the planets.

TECHNIQUE 61 (FOR HUNTRESSES):

Stay Lost!

Huntresses, if your Quarry gets lost, bite your tongue until it bleeds if you must, but do not suggest he ask for directions.

Never take it upon yourself to ask a stranger yourself while he sits there feeling like a lamebrain. *Never.*

Even when a male driver is hopelessly lost, he seems consti-tutionally incapable of sticking his head out the window and asking, 'Excuse me, could you tell me where ...?' God bless the woman who shouts over his humiliated head to a stranger, 'Hey, we're lost. I think we missed the turn.' A man translates that statement into: 'This yo-yo turkey got us into this pickle and now the incompetent, impotent fool can't get us out.' Huntresses, if you are looking for the way to his heart, let him find the way to wherever the two of you are travelling.

Hunters, the converse is true for you. When you use the following technique, your Quarry will know she is in the com-pany of a rare man indeed.

♥

TECHNIQUE 62 (FOR HUNTERS):

Just Ask!

Hunters, if you get lost, do the lady a favour. Lock your ego in the glove compartment along with the maps. Just roll down the window and ask directions.

It won't kill you.

♥

Chapter Thirty Four
'Please, Spare Me the Details'

As little girls, we women were able to weave great webs of fairy-tale fantasies about the lives of our dolls, while little boys could not ad lib an excuse when caught red-handed with their fists in the biscuit tin. Today, the stream of consciousness for little girls of all ages, from nine to ninety, still runs stronger.

This once again became evident to me just last autumn. I was bicycling along a winding path in Cape Cod, Massachusetts, with my friend, Phil. We stopped to calculate where we were on the map. Just then an extremely attractive couple came bicycling in the opposite direction. They were both tanned, fit, and sportive. I flagged them down and asked the couple how to get to Oceanview Drive.

The woman started, 'Oh, this is a beautiful path. You stay on it for, oh, I'd say, a quarter of a mile – well, maybe closer to a half. On the way you'll see many beautiful trees, some of them overhanging the path. The colours are just starting to change. The path twists and turns a bit, but it's smooth all the way. In a while, on the left, you'll see a big white house ...'

Her male friend suddenly interrupted her. 'Yeah, just follow this path and turn left at the end,' he said. 'You'll hit Oceanview.'

As Phil and I rode off on our bicycles, I could hear sounds of the couple's arguing fading in the distance. She was most likely telling him how rude he was to interrupt her, and he was probably accusing her of being irrelevant and too talkative.

As we pedalled along the beautiful path, I began wondering about what might have taken place if I had been bicycling alone that day and run into the attractive man, also bicycling alone? How might the communication between us been different if he had not been with his girlfriend? I would have asked the attractive stranger for directions just as I did. But then, I realized, if he had given me a short answer, all I could have done would be say thanks and pedal off.

How much more I would have enjoyed having the attractive stranger tell me what a beautiful path was in store for me, how it twists and turns, and then give me details about the changing colours of the leaves the way his girlfriend had. That would have opened the door to further conversation with this attractive male.

When I came out of my reverie, I asked Phil his opinion. Suppose he had been bicycling alone and come upon the beautiful woman bicycling without her boyfriend. If he had asked her for directions, what would he have liked hearing? First of all, Phil said, a tad accusingly, 'I wouldn't have asked directions.'

'OK, OK, that I know,' I said. 'But suppose you *had* to find your way and were reduced to that humiliation?'

'Well,' he said, 'she would have turned me off with all that babbling. Ideally she would have just told me to follow the path.'

'Like her boyfriend did?' I asked.

'Well, yes.'

I was merciless. I persisted, 'Well, suppose she wanted to meet you and keep the conversation going. What should she have done?'

'Blimey, Leil, I don't know!' But Phil could tell from my expression I was determined to find out. 'Well, maybe if she'd added a little veiled compliment, it would have turned the tide. It would change the encounter from impersonal to, well you know, personal.'

'What do you mean by a veiled compliment?'

'Well,' Phil mused, 'she might say something like, "It's a long ride...but you look like you're up for it".'

'Oh, come on!'

'Yes, really,' Phil said.

TECHNIQUE 63 (FOR HUNTRESSES):

Just the Facts, Ma'am

Huntresses, when stalking and talking with male Quarry, keep your explanations short. Shave down the details.

If you want to extend the dialogue and switch into a more personal mode, try a little veiled compliment.

Hunters, do not try this. Getting off the objective and switching suddenly into a more personal mode can come across to a woman as being too forward. Instead, extend the conversation by giving more details.

Then, after you have been chatting for five or ten minutes, it is perfectly logical to suggest a further activity together, like having a coffee.

TECHNIQUE 64 (FOR HUNTERS):

Paint a Pretty Picture

Hunters, instead of worrying about how you can score with a great line when you meet a woman, simply flesh out whatever you are saying. Elaborate, and share interesting details. If she likes your looks, she will love hearing about how something looked, sounded, or seemed. Paint a pretty picture for her to enjoy.

Chapter Thirty Five

'Tell Me
(Don't Tell Me)
About It'

There are a few more ropes to learn in the shaky bridge that spans the perilous communications gap. One of them is discovering how to keep the love knot tied even when your partner is upset.

Hunters, it is easier for you, because you need to learn only one phrase. Gentlemen, when she looks obsessed, angry, pre-occupied, or annoyed, use the magic phrase. Ready? Here it is: 'Do you want to *talk* about it?'

Men, when trials and tribulations come tumbling down on a mate, you are accustomed to clamming up or punching your pal's shoulder and saying, 'Ah, it'll all work out. Don't worry about it.' However, if you give your female Quarry this brand of consolation, a flag goes up in her brain which waves, 'Insensitive man. The brute doesn't want me to bother him with my problems.'

Let her know you are there for her. Even if she grumbles, 'No, I don't want to talk about it,' persevere. Say, 'Come on, I know you'll feel better if you talk about it. I'd really like you to share your feelings with me.' Then the dam will burst. Be prepared to be drenched with whatever is bothering her, but never fear. All you have to do is close your mouth and listen.

Listen the way a woman listens, not like a man. To many men, listening means getting the wax out of their ears just long enough to gather sufficient data and then offering their solution. Women listen to each other knowing that they need to get whatever is bothering them out of their systems. Let your Quarry talk. As her stream of consciousness starts to slow to a trickle, you may probe and possibly offer gentle suggestions to show you are concerned about her problem. But do not feel you must solve her problem. Do not feel it is your responsibility. Do not feel as though she is blaming you. Simply listen.

TECHNIQUE 65 (FOR HUNTERS):

Tell Me About It

Hunters, when your Quarry is upset, beg her to tell you about it. Then listen – like a woman listens. It makes you a more loving man in your Quarry's eyes.

Huntresses, when your Quarry is angry, disturbed, or upset you have even less lines to learn than a man. In fact, don't deliver any lines at all. Simply close your mouth. Respect his silence the way one of his mates would. Men are not accustomed to sharing their feelings, so if you insist he talk about it, you are asking him to twirl his hips in an exotic fandango that he never learned.

Incidentally, Huntresses, there is an added benefit to respecting his silence: you do not become associated with his distress. When the storm has blown over, you will be his refuge from the internal tempest he suffered, not part of it.

You can let him know you are supportive, sympathetic, and definitely there for him ... in one sentence or less. Say, 'Of course you're upset and *if you'd like to talk about it*, I'm here for her.' Full stop. Then just go about your own business. Do not be hurt if he chooses not to share it with you. In his terms, he is demonstrating his respect for you by not burdening you with his problem.

TECHNIQUE 66 (FOR HUNTRESSES):

When He's Mad, Stay Mute

Huntresses, if your male Quarry is upset about something that has nothing to do with you, do not smoke him out of his foxhole. Do not make him feel guilty for not telling you about it.

Let him know you are there if he wants to share, but give him the freedom to burrow in his foxhole until he is ready to crawl out all by himself.

Chapter Thirty Six

'What's the Best Way to Get from A to B?'

 'A Straight Line!' He Declares; 'A Gentle Curve?' She Asks

Another gentle habit of the gentle sex that, unfortunately, drives men stark raving berserk is that she hints at something she wants, or she turns it into the form of a tentative gentle question.

I was on a Sunday outing last autumn with a couple who had just started dating each other. Susan and Jake were riding in the front seat and I was in the back as we headed upstate to see the changing leaves.

After we had been on the motorway for about an hour, Sue turned to Jake, who was driving, and asked, 'Golly, would you like to stop for a coffee?'

'Nah,' Jake said. A little miffed, Susan turned around and looked at me. We just shrugged at each other.

A little while later, she tried again. 'Gosh, Jake, do you think there might be a service station coming up soon?'

'I'm not sure,' he answered.

Five miles later Jake whizzed by a service station with a big 'Fresh Hot Coffee' sign out front. Susan turned around to me with wide eyes and that 'Can you believe this brute?' look on her face. She leaned back and crossed her arms. I could tell she was upset.

Poor Susan. I finally decided I should speak up. 'Er, Jake,' I said, 'I think Susan wanted to stop for a cup of coffee.'

'Well, why didn't she say so?' Jake asked, genuinely confused.

'But I did!' Susan grumbled.

'Gosh, Sue, I must not have heard you.' I could tell that Jake was beginning to think his new girlfriend was a bit moody. 'Of course,' he said. 'We'll stop at the next restaurant.'

Was Jake being insensitive? Not at all. He was merely taking Susan's questions literally. Did he want coffee? No. Did he think a restaurant was nearby? He wasn't sure.

Was Susan overreacting? Not at all. If Jake was ignoring her wishes as she thought he was, she had every right to be angry. But he wasn't. He was just thinking like a man.

Susans and Jakes everywhere are plummeting headfirst into the communications gap on first dates. Many emerge rubbing their wounds and vowing not to go out with the other ever again.

When smart tourists go to Paris, they learn a little French to avoid being shunned by the Parisians. When smart Hunters and Huntresses go out on dates, they learn a few opposite-sex phrases to avoid inadvertently turning off their Quarry.

♥

TECHNIQUE 67 (FOR HUNTRESSES):

Don't Hint – Say It Straight

Huntresses, realize that your Quarry will take your questions literally. When you want something, say 'I want' or 'I'd like to'. When you really mean *I*, avoid phrases like 'Would *you* like to' or 'Do *you* think we should ...?'

♥

Gentlemen, for you the reverse is true. For example, on a long drive with your Quarry, you are dying to stop for lunch. Instead of just saying 'I'm hungry' and making a sharp swerve into the next fast-food joint, ask her if she would like something to eat. She will probably answer, 'Would you?' After you say yes, ask her what kind of food she thinks would be good. Let her answer. *Then* you can make a sharp swerve for the nearest grub.

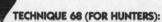

TECHNIQUE 68 (FOR HUNTERS):

Put Some Soft Curves in Your Conversation

Hunters, instead of telling her what the two of you are going to do, ask her opinion first. Also, when your Quarry asks you a question, don't take it literally. Read between the lines to see what she is hinting at. When she asks, 'Would you like to ...' it probably means *she* would like to.

Chapter Thirty Seven

'Could You Give Me a Hand with This?'

What is good for the gander can be ghastly for the goose. Several years ago I learned this the hard way. A friend of mine, George, was at my house helping me with renovations. On that Saturday afternoon he was in the kitchen putting down some new moulding. Meanwhile I was in the living room struggling to rewire an old lamp.

I peered in the kitchen at him sitting dejected and cross-legged on the floor. Poor George was obviously confused as he tried to fit two angle pieces of corner moulding together. He looked like a frustrated child who had just discovered that his Lego toys don't fit. I cheerfully breezed into the kitchen and said, 'Hey, George, I've got a mitre box down in the basement. It will be a lot easier if you use that. Let me go and get it.'

It surprised me that George wasn't too receptive to my suggestion. He declined, saying, no, he could do it fine his way. Thanks very much anyway. I went back to my lamp. At that point I started having trouble shaving the wires. I felt some irritation that George wasn't offering to help me.

Then I noticed that he was putting down the moulding before staining it. Once again, I put on my smile, bounced into the kitchen, and said, 'You know, I have some stain in the basement. It might be a good idea to stain the moulding first. Then you won't need to worry about getting it on the kitchen floor.'

Now, George is a fairly even-tempered chap, but he snapped. 'Leil,' he said sharply, 'don't you trust me to do the job on my own?'

'Well, of course I do,' I stammered. 'I was just trying to be helpful.'

'Well,' he said, his voice rising a few decibels, 'you'll be a bigger help if you just stay out of the kitchen and keep doing ... whatever you're doing.'

'Whatever I'm doing!' I cried back. 'I'm in there struggling with that darn lamp. You know all about electrical wiring. I don't. And you're sitting in here – not even noticing I'm having trouble – letting me fight with those wires. Thanks a lot!' I stormed out of the kitchen.

Bad scene.

Well, by that evening the situation had cooled down sufficiently, and we discussed our little tiff. I brought up the subject by telling George the lamp was fixed. (No thanks to him, I resisted saying.) But I had had a terrible time with it. Then I ventured to ask him why he hadn't helped me with it when it was so obvious I was having a problem. George said, 'Of course I didn't offer to help, Leil, I *trust* you. I wanted to show that I trusted you to do it yourself.'

Like a holy fax from on high, I got it! Of course, George wanted to know that I trusted him to do the moulding job. It is hard to believe that highly evolved and intelligent male Quarry could be so primitive as to invest ego in accomplishing such minor motor-skill tasks, but they do. Conversely, my wanting George to help me was my female desire to have George show that he cared about what I was doing.

It is now chiselled in my brain. Men want to be *trusted*. Women want to feel *cared for*.

Huntresses, until notified, return receipt requested, assume your Quarry is a typical male who wants to be trusted to do everything right. The following advice may sound like anti-feminist lunacy but, I am sad to say, it does work: never give a man advice when he is helping you – *never*. Even if he is trying to fix your leaky tap with Scotch tape and you know seven better ways to do it, hold your tongue.

TECHNIQUE 69 (FOR HUNTRESSES):

Zip Your Lip and Let Him Botch It All by Himself

Huntresses, when your Quarry is doing something for you, even if he is bungling it beyond belief, zip your lip. Unless it's a matter of life and death, force an appreciative smile.

Run outside where he can't hear you if you have to scream, 'Stuuuuuupid, do it this way!'

Huntresses, you have my solemn promise that this way you will be happier and keep your relationship intact. (You can always secretly call a plumber the next day.) Your Quarry will never tell you his affection dripped away because you mistrusted his plumbing expertise. Many relationships have gone down the drain for lesser reasons.

Hunters, you too can glean a moral from the sadly true story above. The message of the story for you, however, is just the reverse of what it is for Huntresses.

TECHNIQUE 70 (FOR HUNTERS):

Unzip Your Lip and Lend a Helping Hand

Hunters, when you see a woman struggling, go to her and ask if she would like your help. Unlike your male buddies, she will not assume you don't trust her to do it herself. She will interpret your help as caring about her and her problems.

Incidentally, Huntresses, you are in for a long wait if you expect your Quarry to offer to help you. If he is the typical male, as George is, he may hesitate to give you any help because he thinks that you would be insulted by such an offer. It is up to you to elicit his aid.

Chapter Thirty Eight
Little Words to Win Your Quarry's Heart

Huntresses, when you ask your Quarry to give you a hand, watch your words. The subtleties that seep up out of the smouldering communications gap are endless. For example, Huntresses, suppose you are at the beach with your Quarry. You pull your sunglasses out of your beach bag and, whoops, the little screw that holds the earpiece to the rim falls out. You look up at your mechanically minded boyfriend and say sweetly, 'Could you fix this for me?'

TECHNIQUE 71 (FOR HUNTRESSES):

Ask *Would* Not *Could*

Huntresses, this is subtle stuff indeed, but say *would* instead of *could* when asking your Quarry for favours. When he hears *could*, the competitive beast hears a challenge to his expertise, not a request for his valuable services.

If he takes the sunglasses out of your hand and gruffly says, 'Of course I can,' you may think he is being a tad brutish. But he has not heard your request the way you meant it. The male brain hears *could* literally as 'Are you *able* to fix this for me?' That's a veiled challenge. It is asking him if he is capable of helping you.

Say, 'Would you give me a hand with this?' It is a subtle difference of one letter, but *would* assumes that of course he is capable, and it offers him the opportunity to be gallant.

Hunters, here are two little words to win her heart and convince your Quarry that you are a rare man indeed. Ask her to sit down before you utter them, because a woman is so unaccustomed to hearing these two words from a man that she may topple over. (And probably will ... right into your arms.)

If something goes wrong in your relationship, or you have messed up in any way, simply say – here goes – '*I'm sorry.*'

Women say these words often, in fact too much. Men never say them. (The last recorded instance of a male saying 'I'm sorry' was in Atlanta, Georgia, in 1907. Upon further investigation, however, it was discovered that the speaker was just a man named Rory trying to introduce himself in spite of having a mouthful of food.)

♥

TECHNIQUE 72 (FOR HUNTERS):

I'm Sorry

Hunters, when you mess up, simply have the courage to say 'I'm sorry.' When you see how your Quarry warms to you, you won't be sorry you said it.

♥

Chapter Thirty Nine

Are There Dangerous Waters Ahead in the Gender Gap?

Hunters, huntresses, we have just viewed the tip of the iceberg of gender differences. After decades of denial, scientists are finally aiming their instruments at the ancient marvel. The deeper they probe, the more they find the glacier extends many fathoms below our consciousness.

Like the careless captain who wrecks his ship on the iceberg, do not wreck your new relationship on one of these sharp gender differences. A new relationship is a fragile boat with the glue still sticky between the boards – it can fall apart at the slightest impact. Every time a new lover hits an icecap in your personality, he or she fears the glacial differences that lie beneath. Guide your new love skilfully to avoid the sharp perils we have discussed. At least wait until the glue dries on your relationship and you are into calmer seas.

Part Six

Rx for Sex

How to Turn On the
Sexual Electricity

Chapter Forty
Your Quarry's Hottest Erogenous Zone

Years ago, whenever you got your nervous little pre-teen hands on a sexy novel, did you furtively flip the pages to find the dirty parts? If so, you are in good company. You, I, and a hundred million other curious prepubescent kids deciphered the same passages.

Well, tell any little kids lurking around your family book-case, 'Here it is. Here's the dirty part of *How to Make Anyone Fall in Love with You.*' This is the section where they will read about stroking, massaging, and penetrating a man's and woman's hottest erogenous zone. They will learn about all the creases and folds of the human body's most erotic organ. They will find out how grownups *really* turn each other on.

However, you had better warn the randy little tykes that they are in for a disappointment, because we are going to make relatively little mention of genitals in this section. To make someone fall in love with you, far more crucial than knowing how to stroke his penis or draw circles with your middle finger around her clitoris is kneading and massaging your Quarry's most erogenous zone of all – the brain. When you have mastered manipulation of that organ, you will have a magic key to make him or her fall in love with you.

Let me say at the onset that the powerful methods I suggest here do not lead you to a lifetime of your own sexual satisfaction with your mate. The techniques presented here are for giving *your partner* ultimate sexual euphoria, thus making him or her fall in love with you. That, after all, is the promise of this book.

Chapter Forty One

No Two Sexualities Are Alike, as No Two Snowflakes Are Alike

We have varying tastes in food, movies, books, hobbies, and holiday spots. In fact, we extol our unique choices in cuisine and cultural preferences. Yet almost everybody is hesitant to tell their partner precisely what he or she would like in bed.

Every month, magazines print sweeping generalizations about what 'every' man wants or what 'every' woman responds to. But not every woman craves having her man weave a rose into her pubic hair. Not every man thrills to finding his woman, naked and wrapped in clingfilm, hiding behind the bedroom door. Our sexuality is as individual as our thumbprint.

General advice on how to be a good lover might work for the proverbial everyman or everywoman. But you are not everyman or everywoman. Your Quarry is not everyman or everywoman. You are in bed with one unique individual, and to make that person fall sexually in love with you, you must throw back the sheets and uncover his or her very special desires.

The Hunter who determines what the bashful child cowering inside his beautiful, sophisticated Quarry really wants will beat out all the competition. The Huntress who, like Mata Hari, extracts the deepest sexual secrets from her handsome, urbane Quarry will have found the key to his heart.

Does this sound like we are taking a trip down the back alleys of sex? Not at all. We are talking High Street, Great Britain, here. We are talking about, if not what goes on behind our neighbours' locked bedroom doors, then what they *wish* were going on. That leaves as many possibilities as there are men and women in the world.

Some like it tough, some like it tender. Some like it raucous, some like it refined. Some like it crude, some like it considerate. The variety of desires that falls within the range of absolute utter consummate normal is astounding. Visions of movie stars, our lover's best friends, twosomes, threesomes- foursomes-moresomes, dominatrixes, handsome rapists, and even an occasional German shepherd normally enter normal people's normal fantasies.

I came upon this awareness quite by accident back in the 1970s when I founded The Project. The Project was a New York State not-for-profit corporation created for the purpose of collecting data on people's sexual desires. Over a period of ten years, my colleagues and I examined data from men and women from every walk of life. Because of the unique method of gathering and disseminating information (not through questionnaires, but by having people send us detailed letters and then presenting the findings through psychodrama), many people who wouldn't ordinarily take part in surveys participated in The Project.

We made presentations to organizations such as the American Society of Sex Educators, Counsellors and Therapists, and the Society for the Scientific Study of Sex. Major media like *Time* magazine, *Psychology Today*, the *Times*, and the major television networks praised our work. Because this unsought publicity emphasized the high principles and confidentiality of The Project, more and more people felt comfortable revealing their deepest desires to us. Thousands of letters flowed into The Project, each detailing the sexual attitudes and assets the authors would like to have in an ideal partner.

 ## How Do Men's and Women's Sexual Desires Differ?

How did men's and women's sexual desires differ? Vastly, when it came to their sexual fantasies, and even more vastly in what role they wanted their partners to play in their fantasies.

Essentially, men's fantasies were more extreme and diverse than women's were. Their desires were tied more to specific acts and attitudes. Their fantasies were less connected to the personalities and emotions of their partner. Often men's fantasies involved control, one partner over the other. One of our more intriguing findings was that men can suspend reality during the sex act and get off more on playacting than women can. (Huntresses, this peculiarity will come into play when we share specific techniques to get a man to fall in love with you.)

Women's sexual fantasies, in contrast to men's, were more complicated. Often they were tied to a partner (not necessarily the one they were in bed with) and emphasized the relationship between the people in the fantasy. A woman's erotic dreams involved her partner's feelings and her own physical and emotional responses to what was going on. Unlike in men's fantasies, the mood and the ambience of the encounter played a bigger role for women. Unlike men, women had less desire to share their fantasies with their partner. (Hunters, pay attention: steamy emotions and love entered a woman's fantasies far more often than a man's.)

Why Are Men's and Women's Fantasies So Different?

Why do women connect love and sex more closely than men do? Anthropologists explain it in genetic terms. The female must fight to keep the family together so offspring can grow up well-fed and well-protected.

Sexologists explain it experientially. Like our personalities, our sexual persona and desires are formed in childhood, especially in the formative years between five and eight. During these years, little girls experience more affection than little boys. Mothers, fathers, aunts, uncles, and even Mummy's and Daddy's friends all cuddle and kiss little girls. Little girls sit on Daddy's lap and hug him more than little boys do. It is natural that a girl might have her first erotic feelings while being cuddled.

Little boys are not cuddled and kissed as much. They experience affection in a different way – maybe a pat on the back or a playful 'Hiya, mate' punch on the shoulder. That expresses love to little boys. Little boys even learn to shun affection and kisses in public.

Recently I was walking past a city primary school at about eight o'clock in the morning. A mother came up to the school with two children of about seven or eight years old. She was holding her daughter's hand, and her son was bounding ahead of them. At the front door of the school, she bent down and gave her daughter a kiss and a big hug. The little girl threw her arms around her mother's neck and said, 'Bye-bye, Mummy. See you later,' and went bouncing into the school.

The mother then bent over her son to do the same. The little boy stiffened and put his hands up to shield his face: 'Mother, *pul-eeze* don't kiss me while everybody is watching.' The mother laughed and said, 'OK, mate. Put up your dukes.' They had a playful boxing match for a few seconds before the boy trounced happily along after his sister into the school.

Little girls, when playing together, touch each other a lot. They plait each other's hair or put their arms around each other when they are afraid. Male friends are more apt to wrestle or 'shoot' each other in a game of cowboys and Indians or cops and robbers. Is it any wonder, then, that girls grow up connecting love with kisses and cuddles, and boys grow up connecting love with a little rough play or power games?

Yet More Differences

The most striking difference between men and women, however, as illustrated by the letters The Project received, is not in their actual fantasies but in what men and women want to *do* with their sexual fantasies.

It is curious to note that men's and women's fantasy desires were in direct contrast to their real-life stereotypes. In day-to-day matters, a woman usually likes to share sensitive information and a man prefers to keep his thoughts to himself. However, in sex, many men want to share their sexual fantasies with a woman. Some even have a compelling desire to playact them out with her.

How to Use Differences to Make Your Quarry Fall in Love with You

Huntresses, men connect sex and ego very tightly, much more so than women do. Men's real-world thoughts ('What's going on in this relationship? Where will it go? How do I feel about my partner? How does she feel about me?') all interfere with desire – read *potency*. Therefore, many men have learned to suspend reality during the sex act. If what is actually going on in bed is not hot enough to keep them hard, they let their imaginations do the job. Men can perform better when they forget about the complexities of their relationship with you and give their imagination and their bodies 100 per cent to *raw sex*. Since a man is more potent with a woman who shares his sexual attitude and his fantasies, he is more apt to fall in love with her.

Huntresses, here is the plan. First we need to explore raw sex. Then, afterward, I give you a technique to excavate your Quarry's core fantasies. Finally we explore ways to manipulate those fantasies to make him fall in love with you.

How, Hunters, concerning technique, women love you harder when you give them fireworks with their sex, but they are hesitant to tell you how to do it better for fear of hurting your ego. Concerning their fantasies, women are more content enjoying them in the privacy of their own minds. Also, when it comes to choosing a lifetime partner, a woman is more susceptible to falling in love with – and getting hot over – a man who fulfils her relationship fantasies as well. The two, technique and relationship, put together add up to *steamy sensuality*.

Hunters, here is the plan. In this section, you will find hot guidance in the 'how-to' department and techniques to excavate your Quarry's relationship fantasies. Mix the two so you can give your woman the steamy sensuality she craves.

Even though everyone's sexuality is as personalized as a thumbprint, there are basic *gender differences* in how men and women look at sex. Before we aim the telescope at your Quarry's one-of-a-kind sexual needs, let us gaze at the universe of similarities.

The following chapter includes some generalizations, to be sure, but we need a solid foundation of basic sexual gender differences before we can get a good footing to explore the unique terrain of our particular Quarry's desires.

Chapter Forty Two

Forget the Golden Rule between the Sheets

The golden rule tells us, 'Do unto others that which you would have done unto you.' Good advice with your co-workers nine-to-five in the daytime and with your friends five-to-nine in the evening. But after you bring in the dog, put out the cat, switch off the lights, and hop into bed with your lover – *forget it!*

The Golden Rule causes big problems in sex. All too often a man has sex with a woman the way a man likes it (sometimes too crude, too quick, too unromantic) and a woman makes love to a man the way a woman wants it (sometimes too slow, too romantic, too emotional). Once you are under the covers with the opposite sex, discard the Golden Rule like a dirty Kleenex. To sexually enrapture and capture your Quarry, a woman should have sex with a man the way a *man* wants it. A man should make love to a woman they way a *woman* wants it.

We have all read that men like it hot and sexy and women like it more passionate and loving. Why, then, the minute the lights go out, do we instinctively fall back on the Golden Rule? Why do we insist on doing unto the other what we most want done unto us – instead of giving our Quarry what he or she wants?

Obviously, reading sex manuals and popular books that highlight, emphasize, and underscore our differences has not done the trick. Men continue turning women off with their unromantic triple-X approaches. And women continue exasperating or boring men with their soft G needs.

Here is help.

 ## Men in Lust, Women in Love

Hunters, the last time you crooned the favourite male refrain, 'Was it good for you too, my love?' she probably murmured, 'Mmm, it was great.' But did she mean it? She might have been thinking, 'Sure, all five minutes of it,' or worse, 'What a snore.' Maybe she secretly wished you had been noisier or quieter, pushed harder or softer, been rougher or more gentle, talked more or talked less. Maybe she hoped you would touch her in the spot where it *really* feels good, not the spot where you *think* it makes her feel real good.

She probably didn't tell you. Don't blame her. She knows you have got a lot of ego invested in sex, and she did not want to hurt you. Furthermore, if she is like most women, she had a fantasy running through her mind to enhance her own pleasure while you were happily thrusting away. Perhaps you were the star of her concealed fantasy film. Then again, perhaps not. But even if she did have you cast in the lead role, in her imagination she probably had you thinking, saying, or doing something other than what you were thinking, saying, or doing.

For generations women were cool to the idea of sexual fantasies. Then, suddenly, in the seventies and eighties, the subject warmed up and became very hot when author Nancy Friday published several sizzling books of women's fantasies. By the early 1990s, it was well accepted that women fantasized. Sexologists and mainstream sex education videos even endorsed fantasy and spelled out the different bedtime desires of men and women. They told us clearly that both sexes like it hot and loving, but men generally like it more hot than loving, while women like it hot *and* loving.

Books were written detailing how to make love to a woman and explaining how different Ms Venus was from Mr Mars when they made terrestrial visits under the sheets. Did men read them? Yes. Did men heed them? No – at least not if you hear the same testimony I do. The women I have counselled and spent hours interviewing ask the same question: 'Why can't a man make love in a way that really satisfies me?' Many of these women are fed up with faking the Big O.

As we approach the second millennium, men have explored the surface of the moon, but the terrain of a woman's body still boggles them. Most men still don't know how to completely satisfy a woman sexually. Yet men *want* to be good in bed. They *want* to give pleasure to their partners. Satisfying their women is a matter of pride for men. Hunters of love, being a good lover is a big factor in making a woman fall for you.

What is a man to do?

Chapter Forty Three

Hunters, Make Love to a Woman as a Woman Wants It

Let me preface this by saying that I suffer no delusions that a few more paragraphs detailing what women want in bed is going to change male habits for womankind. Even the sex manuals' explicit diagrams have not taught men how to gently massage her hot spot. The overwhelming evidence that women crave caressing, romance, passion, sensitivity, and strength in bed has not changed the often rabbit-like habits of the American male.

The reports are in. The cry is out. Men need more help. More drastic measures are called for. If, after carefully reading books like *How to Make Love to a Woman* and *How to Satisfy a Woman Every Time*, the average American male is still thrusting away for twelve minutes or less, he needs more help. Here it is.

The One-Hour Lesson That Will Change Your Life

A picture is worth a thousand words. A moving picture is worth a thousand still pictures. Men, do your maths. The hour-long experience I am about to suggest will be worth a million words to you.

The human brain can quickly forget what it reads, but a moving picture, a video, takes a much longer time to slip out of your memory bank. If the film is hot enough, the images may blaze in your brain forever. Gentlemen, if you want to become a better lover, you have a unique advantage over your grand-fathers, fathers, and even your older brothers. There is a new strain of womankind out there, and she is making her own moving pictures.

If books have not educated you, female porn will sock it to you! *Fem-porn* shows the world what is what in female erotica. Unlike male porn, women's films show you how a woman likes to be kissed and how she likes to be caressed, talked to, and made love to.

What are the films like? You might call most of them roman-tic soft-X porn, but they are not soft because of censorship. There are no oppressive laws, no uptight prudishness, no interior repression. The female directors hold nothing back. Romantic soft-X is the way a woman likes it, in her films and from you.

Some of the films are good. Some are mediocre. Some are downright stupid. But they all contain elements women can relate to. Women's sex movies, in contrast to men's, are more complicated. In place of raw sex, there is steamy sensuality. The films show an emotional connection between the partners, and affection. Close-ups on faces reflect the partners' feelings. (Take notes, gentlemen: you can turn a woman on during sex by your facial expressions.) Importantly, you can see where to touch a woman and how she likes to be caressed. What you will view is a far cry from the misinformation you get from men's pornography.

Recently, in reviewing some male porn for this book, I had to laugh. A male porn star, obviously smug about the pleasure he thought he was giving his partner, was vigorously grinding the poor girl's clitoris back into her body with his middle knuckle. Luckily, for her, he was missing his mark by a quarter of an inch, or her pain would have been excruciating. Gentlemen, the benefits of viewing women's porn don't stop at geography. You will pick up other practical hints, like suave ways to slip on your condom.

Ask for work by directors such as Candida Royalle, Gloria Leonard, and Deborah Shames, to mention only a few of the prominent women film-makers. Here is a preview of coming distractions. In Candida Royalle's films, you will master techniques on how to touch and caress a woman. In Gloria Leonard's, you will find that humour and sex mingle. In Deborah Shames' films, you will learn more about creating just the right atmosphere to make your Quarry fall in love with you.

From all of these women's films you will learn that humour, romance, a build-up of tension, and strong, slow hands are what work with women. You will learn how your Quarry really likes you to give it to her between the sheets – or on the dining room table, or in the lift, or on the beach.

In one vignette, for example, you will see a woman emerging from a bubble bath with a bored expression on her face because she must attend a gala charity ball. She reaches into her lingerie drawer to pull out a white lace teddy. Just as she is tying the tiny satin bow, protective arms encircle her from the rear. She feels a tender kiss pressing on the back of her neck. Sure hands delicately untie the little pink ribbon, her teddy drops to the floor, and the silent stranger lovingly traces a pattern around her nipple with his strong, sensitive pinkie.

At this point, gentlemen, you may be tempted to fast forward to the 'good part'. Don't, because the beginning of the film which establishes the locale, the story line, and the character development – much of this *is* the good part for women.

Many women tie sex tightly to love, and they become fully aroused only when they feel deep affection or respect for their partner. That, too, is clear in many of the female sex films. My male friends sometimes complain, 'Why can't women forget this romance thing during sex and get down to the nitty-gritty?' Well, gentlemen, the nitty-gritty for her *is* love, or at least a relationship. Loving you makes her hotter. Your loving her makes her hotter still.

All the studies prove that women do indeed like more romance. In a typical study, a psychologist at Louisiana State University read men and women the same erotic story. Afterward the subjects were questioned. Men remembered the hot action part where the woman 'clawed at her partner's back and wrapped her legs around him', whereas women remembered as the hot parts of the story scenes in which 'they looked deeply into one another's eyes'.

In men's porn, everyone is stacked, everyone is eager, and everyone comes. In fem-porn, everyone is loving, everyone is sensitive, and everyone is passionate. By watching sex films directed by women, you will finally get it. You will see with your own eyes how to make love to a woman the way *she* likes it.

Hunters, if the written word has failed – if just reading *make it last* has not driven the point home – try fem-porn. Watching the extended cinematic build-up to the sex might just do the trick. It will slow down your foreplay and build up your technique.

♥

TECHNIQUE 73 (FOR HUNTERS):

Learn Steamy Sensuality from Lady Porn

Hunters, there is a new breed of woman out there, and she's letting the world know what is hot – and what is not – for her between the sheets.

To drive your Quarry wild in bed, trash your men's triple-X movies. You won't learn anything from those but misinformation you already have. Pop some films by female *artistes* in your VCR.

Then take copious notes.

♥

Gentlemen, if your good friend runs the video store and you think he would laugh if you asked for sissy titles like *Christine's Secret* or *A Taste of Ambrosia*, the next best thing to do is order by mail. Several 'Better Sex Videos' are very well done – more clinical – but also present material through a soft female lens.

 ## Another Crash Course in Steamy Sensuality for Men

Gentlemen, if you don't have a vcr, all is not lost. Another graphic crash course in turning a woman on is found not in sex manuals, not in how-to books, but in hot novels, female style.

Do you know twenty-five million readers regularly buy romance novels? The most renowned are published by Harlequin in the States, and Black Lace in the UK. If you think only dimwitted women get off on the Black Lace-type fantasies, you are wrong. The majority of romance readers are college-educated and earn an average of £30,000 per year. Each month, 150 new titles roll off the presses filled with hunks like the strong silent stranger, the tycoon who flips his priorities when he meets the love of his life, and even Mr Mum.

Hunters, go to your local bookshop. Mumble to the bookshop salesperson something about, er, you're buying this for your, um, er, sister. Then settle down for an hour or so of very educational reading.

Here is just a taste of what you will find in one Harlequin romance novel.[46] The heroine is Emma, a celebrity author who must stay in an isolated beach house to collaborate on a screenplay with 'talented sexy-as-sin Sam Cooper.' After much avoidance of Sam, Emma decides to have sex with him, but no involvement. Emma is ready, but Sam says, 'I'm not a barn-yard animal! I don't perform on command ... Let's ... let's talk.'

Emma says,

'Look. The smartest thing you ever said was, "it's just sex. Let's get it out of our systems and get on with it." Now, what are you saying?'

'I'm saying let's take it slowly. Let nature take its course ...'

'Why?' Her voice tightened.

'It's ... it's more romantic.'

She gave an angry snort. 'Who's talking about romance?'

'I am. I mean, this is not just about sex.'

'Then what is it about? You said that it was just a physical attraction and if we slept together it would go away. So let's just sleep together.'

'It's not just a physical attraction. Not for me.' His voice softened with a deeper, meaningful note. 'I feel something for you. I think I'm falling in love.'

Hunters, do you pick up that handsome, masculine, sexy Sam is mouthing the sentiments that women traditionally feel? He wants to *talk*, he wants it more *romantic*, and he thinks he is falling in *love*.

Emma, afraid of her emotions, tries to escape.

Desperate, she turned and bolted out the open sliding door onto the deck. A dark gray curtain of rain slammed into her, drenching her instantly as she leaped toward the railing, intending to swing over and drop into the shallow water where waves crashed and foamed on the shingle four feet below.

Strong hands grabbed her by the waist, hauled her back down and turned her around.

'For God's sake, you've got this all wrong!' he yelled above the roar of the wind and the waves, the rain running down her face.

She struggled in his grip. 'Let me go,' she sobbed ...

'You don't want me, you've made that very clear.' She didn't know if she made any sense, didn't care as she thrashed wildly in his arms.

'Does this look like I don't want you?' Sam pulled her close, trapping her against his strong body to stop her moving, and then his hot mouth was on hers, kissing her hard and recklessly ...

'You're a crazy woman,' he moaned. 'You make *me* crazy. I don't know what I want anymore. I don't know what I'm doing. I don't know myself anymore.' He punctuated every breathless word with mad, feverish kisses. 'There's only one thing I know for sure. If I don't have you, if I don't make love to you right now, I'm going to die.'

Hunters, read between the lines and find all the elements. For example, even in these few paragraphs there is the drama of the encounter, the exotic beach setting, and the heightened emotions of both partners. Above all, there is Sam – Sam, the tender man who needs her, who loves her. Sam, the strong, the gentle, the passionate. But Sam's passion was not for sex, it was for *her*.

Now, to the actual sex. When we last left Emma and Sam, they were struggling in the pounding rain with the sound of the waves crashing up against the beach house. They are still there, but by now Sam has 'dragged off her clothing, leaving them both naked to the pounding rain, their sighs and moans washed away in the heavy curtain of rain.'

On the crest of the wave she raised her head. The light from the cabin bronzed his wet skin, sculpting his face into powerful planes and inky shadows. She stared into the startling blue of his blazing eyes, saw the thick, dark lashes clumped together with rain. And then it was upon her, overtaking her. Her head fell back as release shuddered through her, wave upon wave rolling over her, tearing wordless cries and moans from her throat. His hot mouth was on her neck and he jerked wildly, his arms tightening, convulsively as he emptied himself into her for one glorious eternity.

Suddenly everything stilled. There was only the insistent rush of the waves and the rain drumming on the deck, on the water below and splashing off their bodies.

Slowly Emma raised her head and saw his closed eyes, the expression between pain and ecstasy as he crooned softly, 'My darling girl,' running his hands down her back, enveloping her in a warmth that was more than just physical. 'I want to hold you forever.'

Gentlemen, did you notice? During the sex, Sam's feelings, Sam's expressions, and Sam's cries (even Sam's eyelashes!) came crashing into Emma's consciousness through the pounding rain. After the 'one glorious eternity' there was the 'warmth that was more than just physical' and the promise of the future: 'I want to hold you forever.'

TECHNIQUE 74 (FOR HUNTERS):

Read a Harlequin Romance

Yes, Hunters, I am serious. You may chuckle, guffaw, gag, roll your eyes, or double up on the floor choking with laughter, but twenty-five million females cannot be faking that they like this stuff.

Try it. You may not like it. However, you will *love* her reaction when you try some of the techniques that Raphael, Beau, Felipe, Rigg, Sky, Dunstan, Tuck, Kael, Cagney, and other exotic Harlequin Hunters use to trap their Quarry.

Very steamy stuff to a woman.

Corny? Perhaps. But certainly no more unrealistic or wishful thinking than the hot animalistic females who cavort through male porn films begging men to be allowed to do them.

Hunters, memorize a few of the phrases and study the choreography of the moves. Perhaps you think your Quarry is the type of woman who wouldn't be caught dead with a Harlequin romance novel in her briefcase, but no matter how sophisticated or emancipated she may be, lines from the novels work wonders. Hearing 'I need you, I want you, I love you' above the roar of the wind and the waves strikes a primitive pre-lib chord in practically every female heart.

Chapter Forty Four

Huntresses, Have Sex with a Man as a Man Wants It

Huntresses, turnabout is fair play. If we expect the new man to put more romance in his sex, it is only fair for the new woman to put more sex in her romance.

Any woman who has ever been in love knows one thing: love makes good sex hotter. Any man who has ever been in love knows another: good sex makes love hotter. Yet centuries after this discovery, males and females lie gazing at each other across the pillow, secretly wishing the other partner would get it right.

I have said it. Better writers than I have proclaimed it. You can't even slip through the supermarket checkout counter without some women's magazines bombarding you with the message of how to attract a man: Be hotter! Be sexier! Be wilder! Have more fun in bed! Play! If you have serious intentions of capturing your Quarry's heart, yes, you must be hotter, sexier, and wilder, have more fun in bed, and play.

Think back to when you were a little girl, rolling around in the sandbox with the other kids, giggling, wiggling, talking, and building sand castles. You used your imagination to have fun.

Little girls in the euphoria of the moment, throwing sand in the air and shouting 'Whee!' are not having an inner dialogue with themselves. They are not asking themselves, 'Does my playmate really like me? Is he just using me to build sand castles? Should I fake having more fun? Is he expressing enough affection? Why doesn't he shout "Whee" too? Isn't he enjoying it? Uh-oh, will he play in the sandbox with me when we get back to the city?'

Children, lost in a wonderland of sensual pleasure, let their imaginations run wild. They turn their concerns off and their fantasies on. Well, bed is the adult sandbox – the place to giggle, wiggle, talk, and build fantasy castles. It is the place to let your imagination run wild. Bed is the place to turn your concerns off and your fantasies on.

One of the more surprising gender differences is that, during sex many men retain this childlike quality. Like Alice lost in Wonderland, a man can get lost in fantasyland. He is better able to suspend reality and tune into his erotic imagination – not because he has a greater imagination, but because his concerns interfere with his pleasure and potency.

Huntresses, this does not mean that men do not crave caring, affection, and love, but when the bedroom door is closed and the lights go down, he wants to lose himself in total sensuality, i.e. have raw sex. 'Curiouser and curiouser', as Alice would say, is the fact that after several great sessions of raw sex, when no love was spoken of, a man's thoughts are more apt to turn to love.

How can Huntresses express raw sex? Again, perhaps the avalanche of books and articles falling on our heads has not made a dent in our hairstyles. And again, a moving picture is worth a million words.

Let's Go to the Videotape

The videotapes in question are called porno flicks. They are filthy, they are disgusting, and they are a priceless crash course in raw sex. Every intelligent woman should suspend judgment, firmly plant her tongue in her cheek and her derrière on the couch to watch just one.

How do you get hold of a porno flick? You venture into the back room of practically any video store in America. (If you must, don a man's trench coat first and pull his rain hat down over your face.) You will find a wide selection to augment your education.

Obviously, you must be careful in your choice. Porn films come in hundreds of flavours, straight and kinky, with every possible combination of men and women possible. (Sometimes even dogs, horses, and goats play cameo roles.) For educational purposes, you want to pick a 'straight' one. Be forewarned, however, that strictly vanilla 'straight' sex can involve two or more women with one man, or two men and three women. Don't worry about it. The edifying experience will come from the atmosphere of raw sex.

You will pick up hot hints from the female stars who are moaning, groaning, wiggling, pouting their lips, and flipping their tongues in the air.

Yet another benefit from men's porno films – you will pick up fashion tips. You will see the very latest in teddies, garter belts, stockings, negligée, crotchless knickers, nippleless bras, corsets, G-strings, and the occasional leather catsuit or French maid's outfit. I don't suggest you rush out to buy this suggestive couture. But if your Quarry should someday surprise you with a little X-rated birthday gift, recognizing it could save you from a relationship-straining groan, 'What the heck is this?'

What other instructional material is contained therein? Choreography. You will definitely discover some new sex positions. On the average, in each porno flick, the film stars assume from five to twenty-five different positions.

Storywise, you may ask, what are porno films like? Well, not much. After you put the cassette in, you will think you have skipped the beginning because, in less than thirty seconds, you

A Comparison of Female Porn and Male Porn

Female Porn Stars
Strong, sensitive men. Respectful, yet recklessly passionate.

Female Porn Script
Sensitive conversation. More complete sentences than in male pornography, including phrases like, 'You are beautiful', 'I want you', 'I love you', and 'I've dreamed of a woman like you all my life.'

Female Porn Story Lines
Being seduced by a handsome stranger. Making love in danger of getting caught. Many variations on the fantasy of 'being taken'. (They don't call it *rape*.)

Female Porn Locales
Old castles, beautiful beaches, exotic islands. Expensive brass or period four-poster beds.

Female Porn Flavour
Undiluted vanilla.

Female Porn Ending
Fades slowly out on the final kiss after a mutually fulfilling experience. Soft music under credits.

Male Porn Stars
Hot women. Hotter women. Hottest women. (The only place the directors want depth in a woman is in her cleavage.)

Male Porn Script
'Oh yeah.' 'Pump harder.' 'Don't stop.' 'Yeeeeeees!' (Never more than three to five consecutive words.)

Male Porn Story Lines
Ranges from very weak to none. Usually, Dicky sees Jane. Dicky does Jane in five to twenty-five positions. (Huntresses, for a real hoot, put your vcr on fast forward and watch Dicky and Jane do it at the speed of light.)

Male Porn Locales
Cheesy rooms. Any bed, any couch, any floor.

Male Porn Flavour
Every flavour in the book – and then a few nobody ever heard of.

Male Porn Ending
Male star climaxes. (Must end at this point because male performer loses his 'talent'. Film flickers and screen flashes to black.

are into heavy action. You have not missed a thing. There is very little buildup, hardly any plot, no character development, and little personality appreciation. Sort of the way some men like sex? (That is unfair.)

Obviously, Huntresses, I am not suggesting that you emulate the lascivious expressions and corporeal contortions of the female porn stars while making love with your Quarry. But simply having seen a porno flick gives you a more masculine insight into raw sex. The closer a woman is in tune with a man sexually, the hotter sex is for him.

TECHNIQUE 75 (FOR HUNTRESSES):

Learn 'Raw Sex' from Men's Flicks

Huntresses, you may laugh (you may also turn green and gag), but study men's porno flicks to pick up some hints on raw sex. Men spend millions of dollars annually to see hot women lusting after the male body in such films.

You don't have to go overboard and act like you would have an orgasm if your Quarry so much as kissed you, but, to make him fall in love with you, a little lust wouldn't hurt.

Additional 'Coarse' Materials for Your Raw Sex Curriculum

Huntresses, if you don't have a VCR, all is not lost for you, either. You can get a good cross-gender experience by grabbing a handful of men's magazines like *Penthouse* and *Playboy* from the racks of magazine stores. Turn to the letters section, the most educational part for women by far.

In men's fantasies, instead of 90 per cent buildup and 10 per cent sex, you will find 10 per cent buildup and 90 per cent sex.

Instead of reading about the eyes, profile, or bronzed skin mentioned in the Harlequin fantasy, men make frequent reference to their own favourite anatomical part – embellished by adjectives like *large*, *huge*, *immense*, *enormous*, and *massive*.

Instead of Harlequin's sensitive available partners falling in love, the starring characters of men's fantasies are usually unavailable women who couldn't care less about relationships – the naughty nurse, the horny housewife, the hot baby-sitter, the lascivious lesbian, the pantiless hitchhiker. In fact, in perusing a thigh-high stack of men's magazines, the three little magic words, 'I love you', or tender phrases like 'My darling girl' were nowhere to be found. Replacing them were tributes such as 'You're one hot little number' and 'Oh you insatiable bitch!'

Obviously, love and sex are not as intertwined in male fantasies.

TECHNIQUE 76 (FOR HUNTRESSES):

Read Their Rags

Huntresses, read a few men's magazines. You will find the hot letters from hot readers of special interest.

If what goes on in those letters is not precisely true, it is the best documentation of male wishful thinking ever printed.

Chapter Forty Five

A Quiz: Who Loves More, Men or Women?

Hunters, you do (I hope) realize that the generalizations (many), the exaggerations (slight), and the humour (weak) in the previous chapter were simply to make a point. Lest you think I was man-bashing, let me now offer you a peace offering.

Men suffer a bad rap for being less romantic than women. Naturally, if you do a survey of men or women at the mall asking 'Who's more romantic?' the majority will say women.[47] At first glance, the evidence is pretty overwhelming that women are the romantics. Indeed, they are when it comes to saying 'I love you', remembering Valentine's Day, and knowing 'it's the little things that count' (like an engagement ring). But when it comes to the truly deep and important definition of romance, you men are the big winners.

At some point in your life, gentlemen, the woman of your dreams will probably say accusingly (in response to one of your everyday 'insensitive' remarks) that 'you men are all alike! You're so *unromantic*!' My gift to you is the following. Someday it will come in handy, in self-defence. I've packaged it neatly in the form of a quiz that you can give her when she calls you unromantic.

Who really is capable of loving more, men or women?

Questions	Men	Women
Who falls in love faster?	☐	☐
Who is more idealistic about love?	☐	☐
Who usually initiates the breakup?	☐	☐
Who suffers more from a breakup?	☐	☐
Who loves their lovers more?	☐	☐

Who Falls in Love Faster? Men!

In one study, seven hundred young lovers were asked, 'How early did you realize you were in love?' Men fell in love faster. Before the fourth date, 20 per cent of men had taken the tumble, whereas only 15 per cent of the women realized Cupid had stung them; 43 per cent of the women still did not know they were in love by the twentieth date, compared to only 30 per cent of the men.[48] Women are more cautious about getting involved.

Who Is More Idealistic About Love? Men!

Another study determined that men had a far more idealistic and less practical view of love.[49] Men were not nearly as concerned with a woman's social position or how much money she made.

More men felt that as long as two people truly love each other, they should have no trouble getting on in marriage.

Who Usually Initiates the Breakup? Women!

A group of Harvard scientists vigilantly followed the affairs of 231 Boston couples. Of those who split up, usually it was the woman who suggested the separation. The men wanted to stick it out to the bitter end.[50]

Who Suffers More from a Breakup? Men!

The men felt lonelier, more depressed, unloved, and least free after a split. The men reported that they found it extremely hard to accept that they were no longer loved and that she had really gone.

What disturbed them most was that they felt there was nothing they could do about it. They were plagued with the hope that if only they had said the right thing ... done the right thing ...

In fact, three times as many men commit suicide after a disastrous love affair as women.

Who Loves Their Lovers More? Men!

Men love their lovers more in relation to others in their life. Several researchers at Yale University polled male and female participants from age 18 to 70 and asked, 'Who do you like, and who do you love, most in your life?'[51] The choices were lover (or spouse), best friend, parents, and siblings.

Men, it turned out, loved *and* liked their lovers more than their best friends, whereas, with women, the rankings were about equal. Many women liked their best friends more than they liked their lovers!

Gentlemen, the next time your lover complains, 'You men are so unromantic', just show her these statistics and say, 'Yeah, who says? Huh, huh, *huh?*' (On second thought, just say, 'You know, dear, you have a good point. I'm sorry. I'll try to be more romantic. I love you.')

Chapter Forty Six

Your Quarry's Sexual Desires Are as Individual as a Thumbprint

Hunters, Huntresses, let me slap a discreet warning label on my previous recommendation of watching porn flicks. You might get the idea that every man wants a wanton woman slithering all over his body and every woman wants to be swept away and seduced by a handsome stranger on Tahiti's shores. Not true. As with so many aspects of life, just when you think you have got the solution, you find the exception. When it comes to sex, the exception is more common than the rule. *No two people are alike sexually.*

I learned this the hard way, the first time I fell in love, even before The Project's research confirmed the tremendous diversity in sexual desires. Some years ago, I was visiting an art gallery in Chicago. Christopher also happened to be visiting the Windy City that day, installing a show of his own art. I first spotted him across the room, hanging a curious abstract canvas on the wall. I was instantly attracted to him. Everything about him fitted my Lovemap. He was artistic, sensitive, and brilliant, and he had lovely, lovely buns.

We met, we hit it off, and fortunately he was from New York, too. We started dating back in the Big Apple. It was not long before I fell in love with Christopher. Of course, I wanted to do everything I could to make him return the sentiment. My relationship with Christopher was almost ideal. We enjoyed the same activities. We liked the same friends. We both loved going to the theatre, skiing, and cycling. Sometimes we would stay awake all night talking. I felt Christopher was *the one*. As time went by, we fell into a wonderful love affair.

Christopher never said, 'I love you,' but since everything else about our relationship was idea, I guessed our problem must have been the sex. Christopher never lost himself in the throes of passion. He didn't go wild in bed the way I had read a man should when a woman really knew how to turn him on.

Our sexual scenario was always the same. After dinner, usually at his apartment, we would be talking. At some point in our conversation, Christopher would get a cute little grin on his face, put his hand on my shoulder, slide it down my arm to my hand, and stand up. Sometimes he would wink and say, 'C'mon, little girl.' Then he would lead me tentatively into the bedroom. He acted as though he had to proceed gently, cautiously with the seduction. (As if I would say no!)

Christopher's lovemaking was warm and loving, but also predictable and lacking passion. I thought that would change if I just knew how to push his buttons. I decided I needed to spice things up to make him fall in love with me, but I didn't know exactly how.

One afternoon, while pondering this dilemma, my eyes happened to fall on an ad in the *Village Voice* for a three-hour course called 'How to Strip for Your Man'. It promised to 'put some spice in your relationship and drive your man wild'. Just what the love doctor ordered, I thought.

I donned my sexiest underwear and hopped on the A train to a stripper's sixth-floor walk-up apartment in a cheesy suburb. That evening, in her one-room flat, four other women and I

252 ♥ HOW TO MAKE ANYONE FALL IN LOVE WITH YOU

learned how to swivel out of our skirts, provocatively let them drop to the floor, and then step seductively out of them. We got step-by-step lessons on how to slide our bra straps down teasingly, flash first our left breast and then our right, and fling the discarded bra across the room as we gyrated our hips. She taught the more agile among us to stretch out on the floor and teasingly whirl our legs around in the air.

At the end of the class, our teacher went into her back-of-the-room sales pitch. Optional purchases were a cassette of stripper's music and a set of tassels. The tassels twirled amazingly well on the more well-endowed students; unfortunately my equipment was not sufficient to get one good spin out of them. However, I bought both products and, with strains of 'The Stripper' dancing in my head, took the train straight to Christopher's apartment.

I couldn't wait for his cute little grin, because that was going to be my cue. Sure enough, about 10.45, the corners of his lips went up. 'C'mon little girl,' he said as he took my hand and we started toward the bedroom. But tonight was different. Tonight, I had a surprise for Christopher.

The moment we entered his bedroom, I pushed my astonished lover into a chair, slipped the cassette into his stereo, and leaped promptly into my routine. A little fancy footwork around his dresser. One, two, three. Va-va-voom. Peekaboo, one breast. Four, five, six. Va-va-voom. Peekaboo, the other breast. Then my bra went careering cup over cup across the bedroom, making a perfect two-point landing right on his lap.

But my stripping coach had neglected one critical performance skill: it is crucial to keep constant eye contact with your audience to know how you are doing. As I was writhing around on Christopher's carpet, twirling my legs dangerously near his favourite lamp, I neglected to look at his face. If I had, I would have seen a horrified expression.

Christopher calmly stood up and walked out of the bedroom and out of the apartment. In tears, I gathered up my skirt, my bra, my cassette, and my unused tassels and ran all the way home. What had gone wrong?

I didn't hear from Christopher for a week. Finally I called him and asked 'Can we talk?' We met for dinner, and talk we did. He was very forthright. I learned that Christopher's idea of sex was seducing a woman, not *being* seduced. Furthermore, his biggest turn-on, he told me, was not for the woman to be flamboyant and seductive, but to resist. Christopher, it turns out, wanted to feel like the virile seducer. Not, as he said, like 'some lonely repressed guy who pays to see cheap women dance around'.

Wow! What an eye-opener that was for me. I resolved, at that moment, never again to make any assumptions about a man's sexual desires. Every man is different. (So is every woman, and we will talk about that later.) On the surface, it may seem like all men just want one thing but, as I learned, there are many recipes to cook up that one thing.

Sex Is Like a Steak

Have you ever been hungry for a nice big juicy steak? Let's say today you are famished for a truly great one. As a gourmet steak lover, you know there are sixty-eight shades between very rare and well done, but tonight you want perfection. You go to the best steak house in town. You are very precise when placing your order.

You tell the waiter, 'I'd like a filet mignon, please.' You painstakingly describe how you would like your steak charred on the outside, fairly rare, but definitely not blue in the middle. You tell him, 'Make sure it's pink throughout and hot, not cool, in the middle.' The waiter listens patiently until you finish. Then he turns toward the kitchen and shouts, 'Gimme a steak for table six!'

That is the way many of us are about sex. Even when our Potential Love Partner madly hints at some erotic turn-on, we dive into bed with the finesse of a cannonball smacking the beach. Your Quarry may enjoy the sex. You may think it is great, too. But for him, without your understanding of his sixty-eight different shades, the experience is not gourmet. It does nothing for the goal of making him fall in love with you. The saddest part is, he will never tell you why he lost interest.

If you dig deep enough, no matter where you are on this earth, you will find water. Dig deep enough into any man's sex-uality, and you will find a unique twist, a special spin. Hidden in that tangle is the key to his heart.

 ## The Number One Sexual Wish

There is only one sexual fantasy all men and women share. It is to find someone wonderful in bed. Question: Who is won-derful? Answer: Someone who fulfils all our sexual desires, someone who likes to give it just the way we like to get it, and someone who knows how to give it just the way we like to get it. *Without our having to give step-by-step guidance.*

Many lovers are hesitant to map out detailed directions for their partners about their sexual needs. They sincerely believe that 'when the right person comes along, he or she will "just know" what I want.'

I once had a friend named Chip. One Christmas Eve, he and I were laughing about our childhood experiences and how we used to believe in Santa Claus. Suddenly Chip's face fell flat, and he said, 'Santa never brought me the presents I wanted.'

'Not even after you found out that Santa Claus was really your *mother?*' I asked him.

'Nope.'

'Well,' I asked, 'why didn't you give your mother hints?'

'Because,' Chip explained, 'if she *really* loved me, she'd just know what I wanted.'

Most of us are that way sexually. We may not believe it con-sciously, but most people cling tenaciously to the dream that some day, out of the blue, the right partner will sail straight into our lives. And we will live happily ever after.

If these same hopefuls hurled a thousand-piece puzzle on the staircase, they would not expect the pieces to jump out of the box, find each other, and fit together. Yet they dive into a sexual relationship assuming all the pieces will fit. The odds that their and their Quarry's sexual desires will fit snugly together are one in a million.

In the beginning of a new relationship, as all the bits and pieces are still swirling about in the air, sex is exciting. The novelty, the discovery, the conquest carries the night. It is only a few weeks, months, or years into the relationship – when the puzzle pieces start smacking the staircase at odd angles – that sexual disappointment surfaces.

'Why Did He or She Lose Interest?'

Huntresses, he stops calling. Hunters, she suddenly develops other things she has to do on Saturday night. Why? What went wrong? Why did your Quarry lose interest? There are, of course, as many answers to that question as there are men and women in the world, but we can make some fairly accurate generalizations.

A survey we took at The Project asked single and divorced men and women why their previous relationships had ended. Whenever the respondent was the partner who initiated the breakup, we further asked, 'Why? What went wrong with the relationship?' The woman wanted out, usually due to general disappointments in her partner – his personality, habits, lifestyle, or the way he treated her. However, when the man was the one who wanted to break up, sex was pretty high on his list.

The next question in our survey was: 'Did you tell your partner the reason for your wanting to end the relationship?' Overwhelmingly the answer was, 'Not the *real* reason.' The men said, 'I couldn't tell her that sex with her wasn't, well, you know …'

A woman usually wants to go out with a man because he is interesting, attractive, a turn-on, and someone with whom she *might* want a relationship. A man usually asks a woman out because he wants to go to bed with her. (There are exceptions, of course.)

We accuse men of being gun-shy of relationships. This is not true. It is just that if a man is going to commit for a lifetime to one woman, he wants sex with her to be as perfect for him as the rest of her is. The problem is compounded because men's sexual needs are more diverse, more immediate, more pressing, and therefore it is more difficult for them to find a perfect female fit. This is a quandary. Often, a man meets a woman who seems ideal for him, but sexually she is less than the optimum experience. Most men, even today, feel that marriage should mean fidelity.

 ## 'Is This Woman Enough for Me Sexually for the Rest of My Life?'

Roger was typical of the many men I interviewed at The Project. He wanted sex to be great with the woman he would marry but, like for so many men, the fantasy woman he wanted sex with in the bedroom had a different personality from the loving wife he wanted in the living room.

As it happened, Roger came from a very affluent and prominent Southern family. He had high standards in clothes, food, wine, and women. Every woman he dated was elegant, confident, well spoken, and a champion at social graces. He said he wanted to marry a woman he could be proud to introduce to his friends and family and build a life with: 'One,' he jokingly said, he 'could introduce to Mother.'

When I met Roger, he was engaged to a lovely woman named Diane who was everything his family could have hoped for Roger and everything Roger ever dreamed of finding in a woman, except she lacked one thing: sex. There was nothing wrong with Diane sexually. She was loving, willing, and warm. The problem was that, in Roger's deepest hidden sexual fantasies, he dreamed of being in bed with, as he described it, a hot number who was insatiable for his body. Diane was just too ladylike in bed, he complained.

When they were making love, Roger's imagination had to do the work. During sex, he imagined that Diane was crying out dirty words. He longed to hear her in the heat of passion scream out, 'Roger, f*** me! F*** me!' Obviously Diane was not the type of lady to indicate her ardour in this manner, and therein lay the problem. Roger was having difficulty maintaining an erection with Diane.

I asked him if he had ever told Diane about his fantasies. 'No, of course not. It would shock her,' Roger replied. 'In fact,' he added, 'I've never told anyone ... until now.' Roger is ashamed of his fantasy, as are many men. Why?

Most little boys grow up constantly being told no: 'No, don't touch yourself there. That's dirty. Don't look at your sister when she's dressing. That's not nice. No, don't touch Mummy there.'

Little boys entered puberty fearing women would scold them, reject them, if they revealed any flagrant sexual urge – like wanting to hear a woman cry out dirty words. They don't dare ask their favourite woman to play out their fantasy because of what she might think. They dread losing her to some man who does not think such weird thoughts.

A generation of adult men now walking our home town streets grew up terrified by horror comics – not the monsters, vampires, ghouls, and zombies inside the comics, but rather the Charles Atlas (Mr Universe, 1968) ads on the back covers! In the most terror-inducing ad, the wimp (the reader, in his worst nightmare) is sunning himself happily on the beach with his sexy girlfriend. Along comes Mr Muscleman who kicks sand in his face and struts off. With an admiring look in her eye, the poor wimp's sexy *ex*-girlfriend stands up and follows the musclebound stranger (i.e. the man who does it right). Such ads induced panic attacks in millions of men.

Because ego and sex are practically inseparable grey matter in the male brain, if a man wants anything but straight vanilla sex, he feels like the wimp who will lose his girl. Even if he is just hungry for a sprinkling of some exotic spice on his vanilla treat from time to time, he feels Mr Straight-Vanilla will come along, kick sand in his face, and take his lover away.

Roger felt sexually inadequate because he wanted Diane to do 'dirty things' in bed. 'She would walk away in disgust if she knew,' he told me.

'But *would* she?' I asked him. I suggested to Roger that he tell Diane about his fantasies – tell her it turned him on to hear a woman talk dirty in bed. 'Who knows,' I suggested, 'she might even enjoy it.'

At our next counselling session, I asked Roger, 'Well?' Roger had not told her. He admitted he was still afraid of her reaction.

Six months later Roger broke up with Diane. He said that, although he loved and respected her, the passion just petered out. He did not want to spend the rest of his life in a passion-less marriage. Sex, to Roger, as it is to most men, was just too important.

I find this very sad because, if Diane could have accommo-dated Roger's fantasies, two otherwise very compatible people would have been able to enjoy a life together. If only he had told her he fantasized about having a very unladylike hot female between the sheets, Diane might have been able to play his sexual game. She could say the words he longed to hear, and for Roger that would have been enough. Remember, men are able to get off on playacting or pretending more than women are.

Huntresses, you must find out what *really* turns on your Quarry and how to use it to make him fall in love with you.

Chapter Forty Seven

Huntresses, Become a Sexual Sleuth

How do you find out what really turns a man on in bed? Most Huntresses just wing it with what we used to call the *peter-meter*. They try this, they try that, and then they watch his reaction. Some women do their research smack-dab in the middle of the action by asking, 'Do you like this honey? Does that feel good?' Enterprising Huntresses ask, 'Would you like anything else?'

That is good. But not good enough. To turn up the sexual electricity, you must don your Sherlock Holmes cap, grab your magnifying glass, and slink stealthily through all the twists and turns of your Quarry's sexual psyche. You must become a sexual sleuth.

You don't need to blatantly pump him for information. Men are walking lighthouses. Round-the-clock, they flash signals about what turns them on. Yet many Huntresses row their love-boats right into the rocks as though a deaf, dumb, and blind oarswoman were at the helm.

The first step is to develop a special antenna tuned to the right channel – the one that gives off your Quarry's sexual signals. Listen carefully to his everyday conversation. Keep your antenna tuned when he is talking about his childhood, his previous relationships, his likes, and his dislikes. Listen between the words for his attitudes, his emotions. Pick up hints. Most important, develop an ear for any sexual references.

Keep your antenna especially fine-tuned in bed. For example, Huntresses, in the heat of passion, does your man cry out, 'Oh, baby!' 'Oh, darling!' 'Oh, mistress!' or 'Oh, you beautiful bitch!'? These are keys to his sexual fantasies.

With some men, you don't need to play detective. They openly tell you their fantasies. When they do, they are flinging you the master key to their heart, hoping you will catch it. Most Huntresses just let it slip through their fingers. How do you go about erecting an antenna to pick up his sexual wavelength? How do you know which of the sixty-eight thousand different shades of sex he is hinting at?

Everyone's sexual desires are deeply buried in their psyches. Precisely what thrills your Quarry goes way back to his childhood. Whether your Quarry wants you to be a sexy siren (like Roger needed) or a sweet young thing (like Christopher preferred) got programmed into his psyche while he was still riding his tricycle.

Our childhood experiences leave an indelible mark not only on our personalities and our temperaments, but on our sexual desires as well. Just like the little ducklings who got imprinted with Dr Lorenz and waddled after him around the laboratory, any highly emotional incident can become carved into our personal Lovemap. We may remember the incident. We may not. But the experience leaves its sexual imprint.

Roger remembered the source of his desires. He recalls, as a young boy, walking with his father along Eighth Avenue in New York City, a favourite hangout of prostitutes. As they passed, one lady of the night shouted out to his father, 'Hey, big boy, wanna f***? C'mon, f*** me!' Roger's father jolted, quickly cuffed his hands over his son's little ears, and whisked him away into a cab. Roger speculates his father's profound reaction to the words *f*** me* is what emblazoned the experience in his psychosexual memory bank.

At breakfast the next morning, Roger asked his father what *f*** me* meant, and his father, usually very self-assured, became flustered. Roger said that at that moment he felt an intense sense of power over his father that he had never felt before. Power, to a male, is very heady stuff. To this day, that is why Roger responds so potently to a woman using that forbidden word.

Sexual imprinting doesn't stop at childhood. Freud said that there are not just two people in bed – there are six; you, your lover, your mother, your father, your lover's mother, and your lover's father. I would like to expand that list to include a few more people. Every other lover your man has ever had has influenced what he wants sexually. His core sexual appetite remains the same, but desires for new explorations and experiences continue throughout life.

♥ Let Your Quarry Know You Are a Sexual Adventurer

Practically all men want to continue exploring their sexuality. They are tremendously turned on by a woman who is open-minded enough to play.

At The Project I interviewed a man who had recently started dating his girlfriend, Tania. John said their lovemaking was exciting, and Tania seemed open to whatever he did. He was beginning to have serious feelings (i.e. love) for her. One Sunday they were taking a country drive on a long, lonely road that wound through an enticingly private-looking woods. John started to feel those familiar rumblings. He turned to Tania and asked, 'What would you say to a quickie in the woods over there?' John said Tania had looked at him as though he were crazy.

That night, at her house, as they were about to get into bed, John had another adventurous erotic suggestion. He examined

Tania's sturdy dresser, which was just about the right height. Full of hope, he said, 'Sweetheart, why don't you sit up on the dresser and we'll do it there?' Again Tania frowned and looked at John as though he had gone bonkers.

Actually, John said, she went along with it, and they made love with him standing and her sitting on the dresser. But her initial reaction made him feel dirty and guilty for suggesting this unusual position. He never again proposed any other unusual place or position for sex. As much as John liked Tania, this was the beginning of the end of their relationship.

Most men want a woman who will be adventurous and accept their requests with open arms, or at least an open mind. Like Diogenes, forever in search of the honest man, males are forever in search of the woman who will fulfil all their fantasies. Huntresses, to get him to fall in love with you, be that woman.

 ## Uncover His Core Fantasies

To extract a man's core sexual preferences, you must peel back the protective layers he has spent years meticulously constructing around them. It is incredible how we casually ask a man about his taste in food, films, books, music, sports, and hobbies, but leave out the most important taste of all. How often do we look a man straight in the eye and ask him, '*What turns you on?*'

Asking a man what turns him on requires a bit more finesse, however, than just blurting it out like 'What's your favourite movie?' You should carefully choose the time, the place, the atmosphere, and your attitude. The *time* should be a relaxed time, but not when sex is in the immediate picture. The *place* should be somewhere private, but not the bedroom. The *atmosphere* should be conducive to letting him talk, uninterrupted, for a long, long time. Above all, your *attitude* should be playful, mischievous, hopeful.

Couch the question in a way that leaves no doubt in his mind that you are asking what *really* turns him on. Let him know that *anything* goes, and the juicier the better. The goal is to get him to sing like a happy canary.

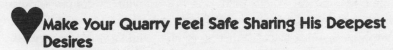

♥ Make Your Quarry Feel Safe Sharing His Deepest Desires

If you want your Quarry to spill the beans, you must make him feel safe giving you an honest answer to the question, 'What turns you on?' Set the stage by letting him know that nothing will shock or turn you off. You will not be judgmental. You are a very open-minded woman and, in fact you enjoy far-out sex stories.

How do you do that? Just like an opening act warms up the audience for the main act, you must warm up your Quarry by telling him a story. Get him in the mood to share his own sexual stories by telling him one of yours – some sexual adventure that happened to you or one of your girlfriends.

If you are telling your own story, make sure you come across as innocent, yet sexually adventuresome. Recount an adventure that lets him know you have a vivid sexual imagination but are not promiscuous. Also, be careful that your story does not hurt his ego or make him jealous. Often it is better to share an exciting sexual experience that 'a friend' told you about. Did one of your girlfriends ever go out with a man who was into a ménage à trois or play a far-out fantasy with her boyfriend? If so, tell your Quarry about it with a jealous twinkle in your eye, as though you wish it had been you who was so fortunate to find such an imaginative lover.

If you do not have any personal experiences to share with your Quarry, let me tell you about a friend of mine named Alicia. I give you permission to borrow Alicia as 'your friend' for the purposes of regaling your Quarry with your sexually adventuresome spirit.

Alicia said she had always fantasized about being 'raped'. Not real rape, mind you, but fantasy rape, a very common female fantasy. Alicia was going out with a fellow named Jim who desperately wanted to go to bed with her. Jim hinted. Jim implored. Jim begged. But Alicia held out. Alicia was a woman of the world and, a trifle bored with her previous lovers, decided she wouldn't have sex with Jim unless she could do it *her way*.

One Thursday evening, after a cinema date, Jim drove Alicia back to her secluded country home, which was miles out in the middle of nowhere. He walked Alicia to her front door and begged to come in. Once again, Alicia demurred. However, this time she said, 'Jim, you can't come in now. Not tonight. Not tomorrow night.' She saw the familiar disappointment on Jim's face. '*But*,' she said, pressing her door key into his hand, 'any night after that – don't tell me when – I want you to ...'

Alicia then proceeded to tell Jim precisely what she wanted. He would drive up to her house in the small hours of the morning. The door would be unlocked. Alicia would be asleep. Jim was to enter her bedroom quietly and sneak past her bed into the bathroom. She told him he would find a condom in the cabinet. He was to take off all his clothes, put the condom on, then stealthily approach her bed.

Alicia wanted Jim to press his hand over her mouth and proceed to tear her nightgown off. She would resist as hard as she could. She would yell and scream, 'No! No! Help! Rape!' Since she lived in the middle of the woods, no one would hear. Alicia would then run for the phone to call the police. But Jim would overpower her and 'rape' her.

That is precisely what happened. Alicia said she will never forget the vision of Jim silhouetted by the ray of light streaming from the bathroom door. Only one thing varied from Alicia's plan. Jim didn't 'rape' her just once that night. He 'raped' her twice. And they made love again as the sun came up.

The beauty of using a third-party story like Jim and Alicia's is twofold. You are not admitting to any wildness yourself that might come back to haunt you later in the relationship, and you are attributing the strange fantasy to the woman, not the man, thus protecting the secrets of other men you have been with. Most important, you are also paving the way for your Quarry to tell his favourite story. In typical male fashion, he will want to play 'I can top that.'

As you tell your Quarry this or your own sexual adventure, watch his reactions. He will probably look at you in a new light. He will say to himself, 'Hey, this woman has an exciting imagination. She's open to adventure!' Not every man wants a sexually experienced woman, but practically every man wants a woman who is turned on by new sexual experiences, especially with him.

As you finish your adventure story, be prepared to handle various reactions. For instance, your Quarry may be wide-eyed and ask if you would like to be raped (or whatever happened to your heroine). 'No, not exactly,' you can laugh. Then wink and ask, 'Any other suggestions?' You have now paved the way for him to feel comfortable sharing his deepest sexual desires. You may come up with nothing, or you may unearth the key to his heart. But now be prepared to hear some of the most common male fantasies coming from his lips.

What are the most common secret male fantasies? Fantasies of having sex with two women, seeing two women make love to each other, watching other couples make love, seeing a woman masturbate, having the woman take charge and give him sexual commands, dominating a woman ... the list goes on. The list also gets increasingly more far-out and esoteric.

If there are any secret marbles in your Quarry's little bag, he will now spill them out into your lap, thrilled that he is with such a free-spirited woman.

TECHNIQUE 77 (FOR HUNTRESSES):

What Turns You On?

Huntresses, purr mysteriously about how you like imaginative sex. Tell him a story like Alicia's, then, with a mischievous little grin on your face, ask him, 'What turns *you* on?'

His answer could be the golden egg guaranteed to get his goose ... and get him to fall in love with you.

The Hot Purr Follow-Up

Huntresses, your work is not over yet – far from it. *Whatever* his answer, feign excitement. Put a twinkle in your eye and say, 'Oh, really?' Then maybe bite your lip a little, trying to suppress your thrill, and croon, 'Tell me more.' Punctuate his monologue with appropriate oohs and aahs, and sexy smiles. Your goal is to get him to continue talking about whatever turns him on.

A few warnings. It is crucial, as he is sharing these intimacies with you, that you don't let one minuscule judgmental frown flicker across your brow. Most women are smart enough when they see their lover's penis for the first time, to know they should look impressed. Well, when a man is sharing his fantasies with you, he is baring his mental private parts. He is sensitive to your every expression. One disapproving look, and he zips his lips on this subject, maybe forever.

TECHNIQUE 78 (FOR HUNTRESSES):

The Hot Purr Response

How should you respond when you get your Quarry talking about sex?

An approving moan, a hot purr, and perhaps a naughty smile punctuated by a little licking of your lips is what X-rated Miss Manners suggests.

Do All Men Have a Sexual Secret?

Get ready for a pretty surprising statistic. Therapists report that about 90 per cent of men have a secret desire they have never shared with their wives or significant others. The *New York Times* reported in a headline that 'Much Is Found Perverse.'[52] We will get to that subject later, but for the moment let's talk about the most common male fantasy secrets.

What kind of secrets do men harbour? Nothing outrageous, nothing shocking. But something that they fear their mothers would tell them they are dirty for thinking – like the six most prevalent secret male fantasies listed earlier in this book.

Incidentally, the *What Turns You On* technique is a splendid method for finding out if you two are going to be sexually compatible in the long run. Some men have sexual habits and proclivities that are a nice place to visit, but you would not want to live with them.

Suppose you are sitting across the restaurant table with the reflection of candlelight in the beautiful wine glass flickering off your expectant, smiling face. You have asked your Quarry, 'What turns you on?' He starts telling you some bizarre activity you could never accept. What should you do? Scream? Grab your bag and run? Say, 'Ugh, that's disgusting!' or 'What a sicko you are!'?

No. Listen anyway. React as though what he is saying is excit- ing. Run to the ladies' room and gag later if it is something you find really distasteful, but now is not the time to show your dis- gust. You have led your Quarry this far down the garden path, and it is not fair to kick sand in his face.

Incidentally, you must never share your man's secret with anyone else, not even your best friend. You have tricked him into telling you, and now you must play fair. Chances are your Quarry's secret will be something very ordinary, but if you want him to fall in love with you, it is up to you to make him think you find his very ordinary desires extraordinarily exciting.

Ask Knock-His-Socks-Off Details Questions

Now is the time to pretend you are in Political Science Filibuster class. This is your final exam on how long you can keep a monologue (his) going. Ask your Quarry every conceivable question about his fantasy. At first he may be taken a little aback by your friendly interrogation. Within moments, I prom- ise you, he will get into the swing of things and be thrilled with your line of questioning.

The number one most rampant secret male fantasy is wanting to be in bed with two women, or watching two women make love to each other. Let's say you have just used the *What Turns You On* and *Hot Purr Response* techniques with your Quarry. Fantasizing two women together was his big confession.

YOU: 'Hmmm. [You purr.] That's exciting. What do the two women look like?' He answers.

YOU: 'Really? [You get a twinkle in your eye.] Ooh. Do they have any clothes on?' He answers.

YOU: 'Wow. [Flash him a cute, mischievous, naughty smile.] Is one of them seducing the other, or are they both into it?' He answers.

YOU: 'Umm. I like that. [Sincere curiosity.] Is this the first time they've ever made it with another woman?' He answers.

YOU: 'Do they have names in your fantasy?' If they do, start using their names.

YOU: 'Umm. [Lick your lips.] Where do Barb and Di kiss each other?' He answers.

YOU: 'Ooh! [You're really into it now.] Are Barb and Di lesbians, or did they just find each other irresistible?'

And so it goes, and so your Quarry's excitement grows. By now, if you are having this conversation over dinner, the table could start levitating due to his growing erection. All right, Huntresses, I exaggerate, but keep the questions coming and you will enjoy the new way your Quarry looks at you. No matter how exciting he thought you were before, you are now becoming much more thrilling to him.

Don't take it personally and feel neglected because your Quarry is talking about Barb and Di, or whoever is in his fantasy, instead of you. Believe me, his appreciation of your open-minded attitude will soon turn his thoughts to you.

TECHNIQUE 79

The X-Rated Interview

As he is telling you what really turns him on, keep your Quarry talking, and talking, and talking.

Pretend you are a television hostess interviewing a movie star on his latest film. Ask your Quarry every conceivable question about his hot fantasies. Punctuate his answers by purring, twinkling your eyes, moaning, licking your lips, and giving him other subtle signs of approval.

Huntresses, you must now get a clear picture of how far your Quarry wants to go with his fantasies. Ask him if he prefers to think about his fantasies during sex, wants to talk about them while making love, or would like to actually act them out. This is a potentially dangerous question because he might take it as his big opener and ask you if you would fulfil his fantasy. Don't say no. Don't say yes. Leave him guessing, but convince him you are open-minded.

In the instance of the two-women fantasy, you might say, 'Well, I've never gone to bed with another woman, but it sounds very exciting. I'd have to give it a lot of thought.' Believe me, you will never have to go to bed with another woman if you don't want to. The fantasy alone will keep him going for years. In fact, many men just *prefer* the fantasy.

 Huntresses, Discover His Trigger Words

Huntresses, we have heard many times that a man is visual when it comes to sex, but did you know he is also very auditory? Like a little kid listening to bedtime stories, a man loves to hear the magic words that turn him on – over, and over, and over again. I call them *trigger words* because they are bullets that shoot straight through to their target. Trigger words aimed at a woman's heart are a powerful relationship booster, but let's talk now about how trigger words aimed at a man's sexual desires are a potent aphrodisiac.

A man can close his eyes to the concrete world of job and family and bills and submerge himself in a universe of sexual fantasy. When you whisper the precise words that trigger his desire, you can propel him straight into another world, and he takes you along with him.

Men love to talk about sex with a woman who will pass no negative judgments. If some men are willing to rack up hefty charges on their credit cards just to share their fantasies with a woman on the phone, talking about fantasies must be important to them. Many men who cannot fantasy-talk to their wives or girlfriends call a sex-phone service to tell a strange woman what turns them on.

What happens in a typical hot talk 0891 number call? A woman with a sexy voice asks (after payment terms have been arranged, of course), 'What are you thinking about? What are your sexiest, deepest, *hottest* fantasies? Hmmm? Tell me all about it.' All she needs is a few sentences from him to get him rolling. Whatever the caller says, the woman pretends to be very excited about it: 'Oh, really? Ummm, I like that.'

A phone-line pro has been trained to listen carefully to her caller's words – to use, if you will, the *Echoing* technique we talked about previously. She makes up a story, a fantasy, using *his* words.

Let's go back to our example of the widespread male fantasy of two women having sex together. Suppose a phone-sex caller said he would like to 'watch two blondes who are hot for each other go at it.' That is all the pro needs. She has her trigger words to give him his money's worth. The call might go something like this.

She might say, 'Oh, you like to watch two women *go at it*, hmmm? I like other women. Especially *blondes*.' (Notice, the phone-sex pro didn't say *have sex*, *make love*, or even the 'f' word. She used her caller's precise phrase, *go at it*.) Her caller would respond breathlessly, 'You do?' 'Oh, yes,' she will answer. 'I've *gone at it* with lots of women. Funny, now that I think of it, they've all been *blondes*.'

Her caller's heavy breathing starts. 'Are ... are ... are *you* blonde?' he asks. When she answers, 'Oh, yes. I've got long blonde hair. I'm about 5´9~,' he gasps.

Now the operator racks her brain to make up a story. After all, the meter is running, and she wants to keep her caller on the line as long as she can. 'Well, it was just last summer,' she begins. 'I spotted Sheila sitting on the other side of the pool. She was combing out her long *blonde* hair. When she stood up

I noticed she was very *tall* and had a beautiful body. I started to get *hot for her*. I walked over to her and ...'

There was, of course, never any Sheila, never any swimming pool, and never any sex between the 0891 number lady and another woman. In fact, the 0891 number woman probably wasn't blonde, wasn't tall, and might not even be a woman. Sometimes transvestites with feminine voices work for the 0891 number services. *But these details don't matter.* It's the *fantasy*, and the *trigger words*, that count with the caller.

TECHNIQUE 80 (FOR HUNTRESSES):

Trigger Words

Listen carefully when your Quarry has shed his inhibitions and is talking about sex. Does he say woman, female, lady, chick, girl, doll, babe? To turn him on, be *erotically* correct, not politically correct.

When he is feeling erotic, does he refer to your breasts, boobs, titties, knockers, kajoobies?

If you want to turn up the heat, forget your ladylike euphemisms during sex. Use whatever words *he* uses.

Your Quarry might not have a sexual fantasy as specific as the one in the example we used, but just get him talking about sex – anything about sex. Ask him about previous sexual experiences. Ask him what he thinks about when he masturbates (all men do). Ask him what would be the most exciting sexual experience he could imagine.

Listen to his choice of words. When he is feeling comfortable, how does he refer to his penis? Don't copy the word he uses when he is in polite conversation. Listen for ,the one he says when he is *hot*.

Sometimes you turn a man off if you *don't* use his trigger words. I interviewed a man at The Project who said he got very excited when he heard the word *screwing*, but his girlfriend always said *making love*. He loved his girlfriend and, of course, when screwing her, he said he was feeling love. But he longed to have her just once say, 'Dear, please *screw* me.'

Huntresses, give your Quarry a rare treat, a sexual thrill he does not usually get from a woman he is in a relationship with. You can do it almost any time, any place – on the phone, across the dinner table, while walking in the mall. Simply whisper his trigger words in his ear.

Give Your Quarry Good Bed Rap

The pinnacle auditory sexual experience for your Quarry is hearing his own special hot words coming across the pillow from you to him during sex. Above all, when the two of you are in bed together, use *his* words, not yours. No matter how silly the words sound to you, if he has told you they are a turn-on for him, believe it.

TECHNIQUE 81

Bed Rap

Huntresses, remember all the details of his answer when you asked him, 'What turns you on?'

Bring those sexual fantasies into bed with the two of you. Make up bedtime stories for him. Be his own private 0891 number especially when it counts – during sex.

Along with the words, invoke your Quarry's fantasies in bed. Find a way to bring up the hot stories he has told you. For example, if your Quarry had the 'Barb and Di' fantasy we spoke about earlier, during foreplay, ask him with a mischievous sparkle in your eye, 'Hey, how are Barb and Di doing?' If this is the first time you are using this technique with him, he might mumble something like 'Er, gosh, I was thinking about *you*, Sweetie.' Then you say, 'I wasn't. I was thinking about Barb and Di. That really is very exciting.'

Talking a man through his fantasies during sex is called *bed rap*. Huntresses, it is not entirely selfless. A good bed rap keeps the needle high on the crude, old-fashioned peter-meter for your ultimate pleasure.

Chapter Forty Eight

Hunters, Do These Techniques Work with Women?

C halk it up as yet another drop in the ever-expanding ocean of gender differences. You will not thrill a woman if, on your first date, you embark on an inquisition about her sexual fantasies. A woman would probably misinterpret you asking 'What turns you on?' too early in your relationship. You would sound crude. Additionally, women are more private about their fantasies and do not feel the same need to share them.

However, you still need the answer to the crucial question, 'What turns you on?' The goal is the same, gentlemen, but the method of getting there is different. After you are into an intimate relationship with her, ask your Quarry (with caution) about previous relationships – what she liked, what she didn't like. Proceed slowly, and let her know your motivation. You are not being nosy. You are so thrilled with the pleasure she gives you that you want to reciprocate by giving her pleasure. Therefore, you would like to know what she has enjoyed in the past. This opens the door for her to give you any guidance or directions if she wants to.

If she prefers not to talk, however, do not press. Step softly, treat gently. If, from what she is willing to divulge, you can pick up some useful information on her sexual attitudes and prefer- ences, you are ahead of the game.

Keep in mind that your Quarry is excited by you as more of a total package. Her sexuality is not as specific. Your technique between the sheets is important but, for a woman, her interest in you runs deeper than that. All of your wonderful qualities and actions, in bed and out, add to her excitement over you.

Gentlemen, whenever I ask a girlfriend what it is that sexu- ally excites her about her current lover, I hear descriptive words like *brilliant, sensitive, responsible, honest,* and a myriad of other qualities that you think having nothing to do with what goes on under the sheets. Those qualities add to her excitement over you, even when the lights are out.

Both Hunters and Huntresses can use another technique to net their prey. Hunters should pay special attention, because this advice is more potent for you. Uncover another kind of fan- tasy, a deeper one which involves your Quarry's psychosexual needs.

Peel Back Her Layers and Lay Bare Her Deeper Fantasies

Hunters, women, too, have hot sexual fantasies – intense sexual fantasies, recurring sexual fantasies. Gentlemen, if you manage to fulfill a woman's sexual fantasies, you have taken a big step toward making her love you. But you can take a greater leap into her heart, a more effective stride toward achieving your goal: fulfil her *relationship* fantasies. As no two people have precisely the same sexual fantasies, so no two people have the same relationship fantasies. Another general- ization, but just as men have more specific *sexual* desires, women have more specific *relationship* desires.

I have a friend named Dana, a thirty-six-year-old, very attrac- tive brunette who has a nightclub act. Her physical beauty outweighs her talent, but she manages to get booked in small cocktail lounges around the country. Dana feels her singing days are numbered, and she desperately wants to get married. Although she meets hundreds of men every year, she has not found her Prince Charming.

I hadn't seen Dana for several years, but we recently found ourselves in the same town. She was performing at a small club near my hotel. I went to see her show and, after her act, we sat down to catch up on old times. I asked Dana how things had been going. 'Lonely,' she said. After all these years, she was still aching to meet Mr Right.

I asked, 'Dana, you meet so many men, and I know a lot of them are crazy about you. What are you waiting for?' Dana said, 'I'm waiting for the right man.'

'Who is the right man, Dana?'

'Well, one who really loves me,' she said.

'I'm sure lots of men could love you. What do you mean?' I asked.

'Well, love me the way I need to be loved.'

'How do you need to be loved?'

That opened the floodgates. Dana spent the next two hours telling me her dream of how someday, in some club, *he* would be there. They would make eye contact while she was singing. He would just stare at her the entire time, never taking his eyes off her. After the show, he would invite her to his table. He would tell her she sings like an angel and listening to her was like hearing the voice of a siren that could drive him to destruction. The phrases, *sings like an angel* and *siren that could drive him to destruction* came up several times during Dana's melancholy monologue. These were obviously phrases that triggered a strong reaction in her.

I began to realize that Dana's description of being loved was very specific, and quite unusual. For Dana, being loved was having a man adore her almost to the point of self-destruction because her singing voice was so entrancing. Dana was indeed beautiful, but her singing voice left something to be desired. To insist that a man love her primarily for her music was a tall order, but that is what she wanted.

Dana and I explored further and it came out that, as a child, her mother used to tell her the story of the sirens, the singing sea nymphs who charmed sailors to their deaths. Dana told me she used to sing in the bath imagining that her toy ducks were drowning sailors spellbound by her beautiful voice. Strange? You bet. But, according to the testimonies I received at The Project, many women have an equally unusual twist to how they want to be loved.

Hunters, you may have met beautiful, accomplished women – women who could have anybody – yet are still alone. They tell their friends, 'the right man hasn't come along yet'. For them, this statement is true because their definition of 'the right man' is very specific. It is important for a woman to be loved *in the way she needs to be loved*.

Recently I decided to add to The Project's research by asking my girlfriends how they envision being loved. I was stunned by the diversity of their answers.

Another friend, Katharine, is forty-two years old and has never been married. She told me she wanted a man who would make her number one in his life, a man who would have no other people in his life who were more important to him. That included even past wives or current family members like children.

Katharine told me she realized hers was a difficult request, because most men her age had been married before and many had children. She told me she had broken up with her previous lover, Bill, because she felt he was too attached to his children by a previous marriage. Katharine knew her craving to be number one was unfair, irrational, but she could not let go of it.

We talked more, and Katharine told me she had come from a turbulent, broken family. Katharine remembered one fearful moment standing in the living room, gripping her mother's hand. Her father was shouting at her mother as he walked out the door for the last time, 'You are not the *number one* priority in my life anymore. Good-bye.' While telling me this, Katharine put her hands over her ears as to shut out the horror of her father's words.

Seeing how moved I was by her story, Katharine shared an embarrassing secret with me. She said, when she was dating Bill, she had an image of herself and Bill's two daughters by a previous marriage on a sinking raft. In her nightmare, Bill would come racing out in a small boat to rescue them, but there was only room for one other person in the boat. Whom would he rescue?

In fact, she told me she once blatantly proposed this question to Bill. He rightfully said, 'Katharine, that's not a fair question. There are different kinds of love. You're the most important person to me in the *woman* category, but how can you compare that to love for my daughters?' Bill was right, of course, and Katharine knew it, but as ashamed as she was of her illogical need, it did not go away. The fact that Bill would not tell her she was *number one* was a big factor in her breaking up with him.

Katharine is now very much in love with a man named Dan, but Dan is more astute than Bill. He knows enough to say, 'Kathy, you're *number one* in my life.' Those words are like sexual trigger words to Katharine. She is hoping Dan will propose to her.

Some women's relationship fantasies are even more masochistic than Katharine's. Have you ever known a woman who always winds up with a bastard who treats her badly? This is such a common phenomenon that some men fear nice guys finish last. With those women, they do. Fortunate women are more realistic and have no strange twist on their relationship fantasies. They simply want a man who is loving, good, kind, and supportive, a good husband and father who will adore them, never look at another woman, and be faithful forever. (Come to think of it, how realistic is *that* relationship fantasy?)

Love Her as She Needs to Be Loved

Women are more demanding than men in the qualities their partner must have. The recurring cry 'There are no good men out there' does not literally mean there are no good men out there. It means there is a shortage of men who fill that particular woman's definition of *good.* Hunters, keep in mind that definition is very subjective.

How close reality matches our relationship fantasies plays a big role in our lifetime happiness. One intriguing study explored how dating couples thought their partners loved them compared to how they *wished* their partners loved them.[53]

Let's say John and Sue were a couple who participated in this study. From their questionnaires, three scores were calculated: how John felt about Sue; how Sue would like her ideal lover to feel about her; and how Sue thought John felt about her.

When Sue believed that John loved her *in the ideal way she wanted to be loved,* she was happiest in the relationship. All the Johns and Sues were happiest when they felt their partners loved them in precisely the way they wanted to be loved.

Hunters, to capture your Quarry's heart, it is not enough to just make her feel loved. Work out *how* she needs to be loved – to what degree, for what qualities. Make her feel loved in precisely the way she wants to be loved. You will beat out men who are stronger, handsomer, richer, and brighter than you. Love and being loved is that important to a woman.

 ## Magic Words to Make Her Love You

Just as using the right words to feed a man's sexual fantasy is crucial, Hunters must use the right words to feed a woman's relationship fantasy. How do you find the right words? By asking, listening, and keeping your antennae always tuned. Pick up signals when she is talking about past lovers, about her relationship with her parents, and about what she likes or dislikes about her various friends.

You might also need to find a way to cut to the core and excavate the kernel you need to plant the seeds of love. Ask your Quarry what love means to her. Choose a relaxed moment, perhaps over a dinner at a restaurant, and then, lightheartedly, tell her you were reading a book about how everybody likes to be loved in different ways – how people have vastly different ideas of what a relationship should be.

Simply ask her, 'If someone fell in love with you, how would you most like to be loved?' She may hesitate in embarrassment, but persist. You will get your ammunition, your kernel. Ten women will give you ten different answers. A thousand women will give you a thousand different answers. You will be stunned at the diversity of the replies, but one thing will be consistent. With each woman, the same words will pop up several times.

Hunters, if you were trying to make my friend Dana fall in love with you, you would tell her, 'Dana, your *beautiful voice drives me to destruction.*' If you had set your sights on Katharine, you would say, 'Katharine, you are *number one* in my life.' Those are the trigger words, the golden keys, to open their particular hearts.

TECHNIQUE 82 (MORE FOR HUNTERS):

Relationship Trigger Words

First, ask her 'What is love?' to find out how your Quarry would most like to be loved.

While she is answering you, listen carefully for trigger words. Do not use them immediately, but when it comes time to say 'I love you,' weave in these special words. ♥

Huntresses, Relationship Trigger Words Work for You, Too

Men also have specific ways of wanting to be loved. However, there is an additional twist you can use to find out how your Quarry wants to be loved. Uncover his source of pride, and use the magic words that describe it.

One man might want a woman who loves him because he is brilliant. Another needs to feel he is sexually irresistible. Still another might yearn to be Peter Pan, who is loved for his boyishness.

A friend of mine named John, a lawyer, recently became engaged. John is very proud that he had brought himself up by his bootstraps. In fact, that is one of his favourite phrases, and I have heard him use it over and over. His father was a street cleaner, and John put himself through college and then law school.

One time John and I were talking about his fiancée, Lisa. He told me, 'Lisa understands that I *brought myself up by my bootstraps* and admires me for that.' I thought to myself, 'Does Lisa really admire that? Or is Lisa a very smart woman who understands that is John's source of pride?'

Once I had a tenant, a handsome young police officer named Karl, who dated a lot of women. Knowing of my interest in relationships, he often told me about his girlfriend-of-the-week. Karl's recurring phrase was, 'I think she really digs my style.' Probably none of the girls he was dating actually said the words, 'Karl, I *dig your style*,' but if one of them was smart enough to pick up on those words, she would be hitting his hot button.

Huntresses, make a man feel you love and admire him for the qualities he is most proud of. Chances are your Quarry has even inadvertently fed you the right words to use on him. Practically everybody has favourite relationship words. John's *brought myself up by my bootstraps* and Karl's *digs my style* were latchkeys to winning their love. Echoing those phrases back is taking direct aim at these men's hearts with your Cupid's bow.

Chapter Forty Nine

Finally, Snaring the Confirmed Bachelor

Every now and then Huntresses eat their hearts out and tear their hair out over confirmed bachelor Quarry – the older, attractive man who is single and has never been married. You have met the type. You would think he could have his pick. He dates beautiful women and he has affairs with them. But his relationships never last more than a couple of months. When his friends ask him what he is waiting for, he just smiles, shrugs, and says, 'Oh, the right woman hasn't come along yet.'

Is this type of bachelor Quarry lying? Is he determined to stay single until the day he dies? Usually not. Usually, he is not lying and, yes, usually the right woman for him just has not come along yet. What he does not tell you is that he means *sexually* the right woman has not come along yet.

Jerry was the perfect example of the man-about-town every-one thought of as a determined, persistent, resolute bachelor. In fact, Jerry was the most eligible bachelor in his home town social scene. He was good-looking, about forty, and very per-sonable. He had an exciting job as the host of a local television talk show. Sometimes Jerry's television guests would even ask him on the air, 'Jerry, when are you going to settle down?' or, 'Jerry, every woman in town is after you. When are you going to choose the lucky girl?' Jerry's answer was always the same: 'The right woman hasn't come along yet.'

Huntresses, if you should find yourself attracted to one of these never-been-trapped Quarry, your mathematical chances of being the one to bag him are pretty low unless you have some special ammunition – special weapons that other Huntresses do not have. Armed with this special knowledge, you increase your chances of becoming the long-awaited 'right woman' for the Jerry-type confirmed bachelor.

I met Jerry while I was directing sexual research at The Project. I was a frequent 'guest expert' on his show, and we became platonic friends. One night, after his show, we were having dinner together at a restaurant near his television station. When I asked Jerry the same question everyone asked him, 'Why hasn't the right woman come along?' he felt he could trust me. He spelled it all out.

It turns out that Jerry had a secret, but he was so embarrassed about it that he could never tell anyone. Wringing his hands between stabbing at his fillet of sole, Jerry whispered his deep dark secret to me: 'Sometimes when I'm in bed with a woman, I fantasize I'm the woman and she's the man. She takes charge and seduces me.'

'So?' I said. 'What's the big deal?'

'The big deal is,' he said nervously, looking around to make sure no one could hear him, 'I picture myself wearing her clothes.' He put his fork down and buried his face in his hands.

'Jerry, it's not that bad. That's a very common fantasy,' I told him. His grateful smile was my reward for my exaggeration. Over the next few hours, Jerry loosened up and told me everything. He said that, whenever he goes out on a date with a woman, he throws out a few hints to see how she might react. For instance, sometimes he would look at his date's high-heeled shoes and say, 'Hey, those are great-looking shoes. How do you think I'd look in them? Ha ha ha.'

Jerry scrutinizes her reaction *very carefully*. If she happens to say something like, 'Oh, you'd look awful!' that actually shuts off Jerry's erotic interest in her. However, if she responds, 'Not bad,' he considers that a good reaction and stays interested in her. If she says something further like, 'Oh, you'd look very pretty in high-heeled shoes,' Jerry says he goes crazy with desire for her. That is how arbitrary some men's sexuality can be!

A Huntress often turns a man off by failing to respond in a particular way to his sexual hints. However, if the woman has no experience or knowledge in the area of offbeat fantasies, she cannot be expected to give the right response.

The kinky stuff we have all read about in the tabloids and heard giggled about on the television talk shows is baffling. Many people think all the men who want to play unusual sex games are a bunch of wackos who should all be locked up. What they do not understand is that it is not black-and-white, kinky or not kinky. Many men have traces of unconventional desires – not strong enough, or desperate enough, to make them go on a national talk show and humiliate themselves in front of the nation, but strong enough to hold out marrying a woman unless she accepts his kinky twist.

Jerry told me that, if his date *does* respond positively to his hints, he takes things one step further. After several times in bed with his new woman, he will suggest one night they do role reversal. 'Tonight,' he'll joke, 'you be the guy and I'll be the girl. Go ahead, seduce me!' Most of his girlfriends, Jerry said, take a half-hearted stab at it. 'But,' he told me, 'I can tell if she's not enjoying it. And if she doesn't, well, I can't help it. Sexually, I lose interest in her. Whenever I find the right woman who enjoys dressing me up in her clothes, I'll marry her in a minute.' He is not joking.

There are millions of Jerrys out there. They do not all want to dress up in your clothes, but they want some very un-vanilla flavours in their dishes.

Why Do Jerrys Want Such Far-Out Sex?

As we have seen, like the rest of our personalities, practically all of our sexual needs and desires have their roots in childhood. Under analysis their origins often come out, but some men do not need analysis to trace their sexual fantasies to their roots.

Jerry remembers one time when he was about five years old. His big sister and several of her little friends stripped him down naked and dressed him up in their lacy underwear. He remembers looking down at himself in girls' pretty panties and seeing a little bulge, his first erection. Jerry was humiliated by being controlled by the girls, but he loved the attention. It scarred his Lovemap forever.

Huntresses, keep your ears especially tuned to pick up hints of fantasy games involving control. This dominance/submission game is the most common exotic bud in men's secret gardens. It surprises many people but the truth is that, between the two, being submissive is a far more prevalent craving.

For women who have traditionally taken a more yielding role, being sexually submissive is no big deal. The classic 'being taken' fantasy – the handsome stranger whisking her away in the middle of the night to his castle and having his way with her – is not embarrassing. However, if a man should have the concomitant fantasy of a strong woman tying him up to the bedpost and having her sexual way with him, he is mortified.

Why are fantasies of control so prevalent? Most little boys experience their first sexual pleasure early in life when Mother is still the centre of the universe. As an infant, Mother bathes him, changes his nappies, spanks him, powders his little penis, and gives him enemas and all sorts of other intimate, unmanly attentions. Although Mother is his protector, she is also his first authority figure, his dictator. She punishes him when he does wrong. He is helpless and completely at her mercy, but he feels in his little heart that he has her undying love. Therein lies a great security.

As an adult, away from the control and protection of Mother, a man is left alone. All of us, whether we realize it or not, are continually searching for ways to cope with this feeling of being alone, of feeling alienated. Some men find solace in their sexual fantasies. If he cannot have Mother back, he can have another beautiful woman to tell him what to do. Not only will she tell him what to do, but she will tell him how to do it, and maybe even punish him when he does it wrong. This type of man seeks a sexual partner who will permit him to let it all out, let him cry, let him beg, let him be a helpless child again.

Some men flip the whole fantasy and want to do unto you that which they cannot admit to themselves they want done unto them. This type of man keeps these fantasies locked away in his private sexual psyche until some clever Huntress rubs Aladdin's lamp and frees his fantasies and makes him feel OK about them.

Huntresses, if you feel you could be happy with a Jerry, there is a sure way to his heart. Simply play his fantasy games. Not all Jerrys want to dress in women's clothes. Other Jerrys want to spice up their lovemaking with games that involve spanking, tickling, wrestling, or bringing some far-out toys to bed with the two of you.

A Walk on the Weird Side

Some confirmed bachelors have even deeper, darker secrets. Like the duckling who identifies as its mother the first moving object it sees once it leaves the egg, some young boys carry throughout their lives an incurable attraction to an experience or object that left a profound impression on them. If a young boy's sexual cravings misfire, they can get tied to the rubber apron that rubbed against his little genitals while Mother was changing his nappy or the bare feet he saw walking around his crib. For some few men, these can develop into full-blown fetishes. Because fetishes are practically non-existent in females, many women do not understand them.

Can you change your Quarry's desires, help him grow out of them? No, therapists tell us. Just as it is practically impossible to change a gay man and make him heterosexual, it is a losing battle to try to change a kinky man and make him go straight. Most far-out fantasies, like Jerry's desire to wear female clothing, are baffling, but they generally fall into definable categories.

Suffice it to say that if you do find yourself interested in a Jerry or some other sexually exotic species, simply make a return trip to your video library. This time, say, 'Ahem, I'd like a bondage [or whatever his kick is] film, please.'

Chapter Fifty

On Looking at Other Women

Let us now surface from the underground to Main Street, Everytown, and a problem that *all* men and women face when they are out with their main squeeze.

A couple, Dick and Jane, are happily strolling hand in hand along the sidewalk together. A gorgeous woman comes slinking toward them from the opposite direction. 'Rats,' Jane thinks: 'I just bet Dick's going to look at her. He wouldn't dare.'

'Va va va *voom!*' Dick thinks. 'What a dish! Whoops, I'd better not let Jane catch me looking at her. Well, I'll just keep my head straight ahead and strike when the eyein' is hot. I'll give my eyes a quickie as she passes close to us.'

Dick and Jane keep walking, nonchalantly, oblivious, of course, to the approaching dish. Dick smiles at Jane and gives her hand a squeeze for reassurance. Jane smiles contentedly.

The dish gets closer. And closer. This is Dick's window of opportunity. It is now or never. He lets his eyeballs swivel her way for a split second. Does he get away with it?

Not in a pig's eye! As far as Jane is concerned, Dick's eyeballs might as well be hanging out and dangling by the optic nerve as the dish passed. Jane goes into a funk or a bout of insecurity, or she hits Dick with an original line like, 'What, you've never seen a woman before?'

Bad scene.

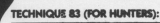

TECHNIQUE 83 (FOR HUNTERS):

No Lookee-Dishee

Hunters, to win the heart of your Quarry, don horse blinkers whenever you're with her. Keep your eyeballs on a strict diet.

In fact, pray that a dazzling dish walks your way just so you can prove to your Quarry how oblivious you are to other women – how you only have eyes for your own fair lady.

Huntress, here is a trick that will help you win the heart of your male Quarry when the inevitable happens. Let me put this in the form of a legal argument.

WHEREAS: All men enjoy looking at other women ... no matter how much they pretend they don't,

WHEREAS: Men love it when a woman gives him permission to do something he really wanted to do all along but felt he shouldn't,

THEREFORE: To win the heart of your Quarry, help him do what he wants to do all along. Give him guilt-free snacks. Point out the good-looking cookies. *Make him look at other women*.

Point out other women on the street, at a party, on television. Search for them in crowds and make sure your Quarry doesn't miss a single one. How much more affection Dick would·have felt for Jane if she had said as she spotted the advancing dish, 'Wow, Dick, you're going to like what's coming.'

TECHNIQUE 84 (FOR HUNTRESSES):

Lookee-Dishee

Huntresses, point out attractive women to your Quarry to give him permission to look at them. Say things like, 'Now, there's a woman with style,' or even, 'Wow, is she pretty, or what?'

If he is smart, your Quarry will probably protest and mumble something about how you are better-looking. But then he will have his guilt-free gander, and you will have a much happier goose.

Chapter Fifty One

The Final Stone Unturned

Never let it be said that one tiny pebble was left unturned in the exploration of *How to Make Anyone Fall in Love with You*. No thorough investigation would be complete without examining another passage to our Quarry's heart – the nasal passage, or pheromones.

What?

Pheromones. Chemical body excretions. Body odours.

There has been much talk in recent years of pheromones. In certain insects and animals, pheromones have proved to be potent stuff indeed. Some bugs just gotta have it when they get an olfactory jolt. And when a female pig gets a whiff of pheromones emanating from a sweaty male pig, she spreads her nostrils, turns her rump toward him, and oinks seductively.

In human animals, sweat, foot odour, and vaginal fluids (the odours that Americans gratefully pay deodorant companies to wipe out) would count as pheromones. Do they work? Do male body odours have the same effect on human females and vice versa as they have on the opposite sexes in the animal kingdom?

Certain humans do openly respond to body odours. Many men like the scent of a woman's underarms. Napoleon reportedly sent a letter to his beloved Josephine imploring her, 'I will be arriving in Paris tomorrow evening. Don't wash.' Today, however, the average wife would be more apt to send her pit-sniffing husband to a sex therapist.

Scepticism aside, some researchers still harbour high hopes for human pheromones. Half a dozen respected scientists think they have discovered a new sense organ in our nasal cavity called the *vomeronasal organ*, or VNO. These scientists tell us that anatomists have overlooked this organ for centuries. No wonder – it is nothing more than a tiny, pale pit near the bottom of the septal wall dividing the nose. This minuscule dent is reported to detect chemical signals passed unconsciously between people.

To prove their point, these scientists did what all scientists do. They conducted experiments. But when their human research subjects lay flat on their backs flaring their nostrils for science, nothing happened. Women who sniffed armpit pads that men had worn for several days did experience a slight change in their menstrual cycles, but they certainly reported no feelings of sexual attraction.

However, modern-day scientists and entrepreneurs, ever in search of a headline-grabbing discovery, continue their research. The hope (and the hype?) is that by bottling a form of human body odours, humans will be able to generate the same reaction as the female pig when she gets a blast of boar breath. One clever entrepreneur has already bottled a new form of the old substance, body odour, and is selling it at fifty pounds for fifty millimetres. Mail-order catalogues have jumped on the BO bandwagon and are advertising secret ingredients from the human body guaranteed to hypnotize and attract members of the opposite sex.

I have conducted little first-hand research in this area, but my own unscientific observation is that, if you dab some pheromones behind each ear, you may indeed find horny female insects flying around your head. No evidence to date proves to me that pheromones can cause the same reaction in humans.

The sense of smell, however, is a powerful attraction. Who knows? There is a whiff of evidence that these scientists and entrepreneurs are on to something – enough, at least, to warrant one final bit of advice: be very conscious of the effects your smell can have on your Quarry.

TECHNIQUE 85

Who Nose?

Do not expect your Quarry to fall nose over heels in love with you just because of your scent. However, since pheromones play an important role in animal erotica, cover your bets. Give your relationship an olfactory boost by letting your Quarry choose your perfume or aftershave for you.

Afterword

We enter this world from our mother's womb, alone. We live our lives in a solitude defined by the boundary of our mind and our body. And we exit this earthly existence unaccompanied. If, in between, two solitudes can find togetherness and communion with another mortal, they find true happiness indeed. But true love is a luxury, not our pre-ordained birthright. As with achieving any luxury, we must examine the most powerful methods to acquire it.

We look to scientific research to tell us *why* people fall in love and then fashion our deeds to meet the needs of the mortal we want to make fall in love with us. But, as the English poet Samuel Taylor Coleridge wrote in a letter to one of his colleagues, 'I believe the souls of five hundred Sir Isaac Newtons would go to the making up of a Shakespeare or a Milton.'

So it is with love. Harken the studies which tell us of the six elements we have explored:

the impact of *first impressions*,
  the influence of *similarity*,
    the skewed reckoning of *equity*,
      the narcissism of *ego*,
        the magnitude of *gender differences*, and
        the joy and enrapturement of *sex*.

Spike your arrow with this wisdom and the techniques that science has spawned. But as you take aim at your Quarry, never forget the artistry, the creativity, and the *magic* of love. A great performer studies techniques for a lifetime but, flooded by the warmth of the spotlight, those gruelling years of practice fade into the past. Triumphant performers give themselves to the moment, and let the magic unfold naturally. So it is with romance. Study and practise the techniques to make somebody fall in love with you. But when the moment arrives, give yourself to it. Follow your instincts and obey your heart.

I wish you love.

Notes

1. Peter O. Peretti, and Heidi Kippschull, 'Influence of Five Types of Music on Social Behaviors of Mice', *Psychological Studies* 35, (ii):98–103, 1989.
2. Jonathan P. Rosman and Phillip J. Resnick, 'Sexual Attraction to Corpses: A Psychiatric Review of Necrophilia', *Bulletin of the American Academy of Psychiatry and the Law*, 17, (ii):153–163, 1989.
3. Harrison Voigt, 'Enriching the Sexual Experience of Couples: The Asian Traditions', *Journal of Sex and Marital Therapy*, 17, (iii):214–219, 1991.
4. Carol Rambo Ronai and Carolyn Ellis, 'Turn-Ons for Money: Interactional Strategies of the Table Dancer', *Journal of Contemporary Ethnography*, 18, (iii):271–298, 1989.
5. Deborah Tannen, PhD. *You Just Don't Understand*, London, Virago, 1992; Simon & Schuster Audioworks.
6. John Gray, PhD. *Men Are from Mars, Women Are from Venus*, London, Thorsons, 1993; Thorson's Audio, 1996.
7. John Money, PhD. *Lovemaps*, New York, Prometheus Books, 1990.
8. Paula Mergenhagen DeWitt, 'All the Lonely People', *American Demographics*, April 1992, 44–48.
9. W.J. Goode, 'The Theoretical Importance of Love', *American Sociological Review*, 2:38–47, (1959).

10. Bernard I. Murstein, PhD. 'Love at First Sight: A Myth', *Medical Aspects of Human Sexuality* 14, (ix), 1980.
11. W.J. McKeachie, 'Lipstick as a Determiner of First Impressions of Personality', *Journal of Social Psychology* 36:241–244, (1952).
12. A.M. Mathews, et al. 'The Principal Components of Sexual Preference', *British Journal of Social Clinical Psychology* 11:35–43, (1972).
13. Joan Kellerman, et al. 'Looking and Loving: The Effects of Mutual Gaze on Feelings of Romantic Love', *Journal of Research in Personality* 23 (ii):145–161, 1989.
14. *Ibid.*
15. Helen Fisher, *Anatomy of Love*, London, Touchstone Books, 1993.
16. Zick Rubin 'Measurement of Romantic Love', *Journal of Personality and Social Psychology* 16:265–273, (1970).
17. Ilkka Linnankoski, et al. 'Eye Contact as a Trigger of Male Sexual Arousal in Stump-Tailed Macaques', *Folia-Primatologica*, (iii):181–184, 1993.
18. Helen Fisher, *Anatomy of Love*, Touchstone Books, 1993.
19. *Ibid.*
20. M.M. Moore, 'Nonverbal Courtship Patterns in Women: Context and Consequences', *Ethnology and Sociobiology* 6:237–247, (1985).
21. Mark Cook, 'Gaze and Mutual Gaze in Social Encounters', *American Scientist* 65:328–333 (1977).
22. Timothy Perper, *Sex Signals: The Biology of Love*, Philadelphia, ISI Press, 1985.
23. E. Aronson et al. 'The Effect of a Pratfall on Increasing Interpersonal Attractiveness', *Psychonomic Science* 4:227–228, (1966).
24. E. Walster, G.W. Walster et al. 'Playing Hard to Get: Understanding an Elusive Phenomenon', *Journal of Personality and Social Psychology* 26:113–121, (1973).
25. D.G. Dutton and A.P. Aron, 'Some Evidence for Heightened Sexual Attraction Under Conditions of High Anxiety', *Journal of Personality and Social Psychology* 30:510–517, (1974).
26. *Ibid.*
27. A.H. Maslow and N.L. Mintz, 'Effects of Aesthetic Surroundings', *Journal of Psychology* 41:247–254, (1956).
28. W. Griffitt and R. Veitch, 'Hot and Crowded: Influence of Population Density and Temperature on Interpersonal Affective Behavior', *Journal of Personality and Social Psychology* 17:92–98 (1971).

29. John M. Townsend and Gary D. Levy 'Effects of Potential Partner's Physical Attractiveness and Socioeconomic Status on Sexuality and Partner Selection', *Archives of Sexual Behavior*, 19, (ii):149–164, 1990.

30. Donn Byrne, *The Attraction Paradigm*, New York, Academic Press, 1971.

31. Elaine Walster, William G. Walster and Ellen Berscheid, *Equity: Theory and Research*, Boston, Allyn and Bacon, 1978.

32. Donn Byrne, et al. 'Continuity Between the Experimental Study of Attraction and Real-Life Computer Dating', *Journal of Personality and Social Psychology*, 1:157–165, (1970).

33. Robert J. Sternberg, *The Triangle of Love*, Scranton, Pennsylvania, Basic Books, 1988.

34. C. Kerckhoff and K.E. Davis, 'Value Consensus and Need Complementarity in Mate Selection', *American Sociological Review* 27:295–303, (1962).

35. Mark Cook and Robert McHenry, *Sexual Attraction*, New York, Pergamon Press, 1978.

36. Brenda Major, et al. 'Physical Attractiveness and Self Esteem: Attributions for Praise from an Other Sex Evaluator', *Personality and Social Psychology Bulletin* 10, (i):43–50, 1984.

37. Elaine Walster, William G. Walster and Ellen Berscheid, *Equity: Theory and Research*, Boston, Allyn and Bacon, 1978.

38. I. Silverman, 'Physical Attractiveness and Courtship', *Sexual Behavior* Sept:22–25, 1971.

39. E. Walster, G.W. Walster and S. Traupmann, 'Equity and Premarital Sex', Unpublished manuscript, 1977.

40. A.M. Mathews, *British Journal of Social Clinical Psychology* 11:35–43, (1972).

41. J. Lavrakas, 'Female Preferences for Male Physiques', *Journal of Research in Personality* 9:324–334, (1975).

42. Jane E. Smith, et al. 'Single White Male Looking for Thin, Very Attractive ...', *Sex Roles* 23:675–685, (1990).

43. *Encounter*, 1956.

44. D.J. Bem 'Self Perception Theory' *Advances in Experimental Social Psychology* 6:1–62, (1972).

45. *Ibid.*

46. Debra McCarthy-Anderson and Carol Bruce-Thomas, *Obsession*, Ontario, Canada, Harlequin Books, 1995.

47. Results of public opinion polls. *The American Enterprise*, Jan–Feb 3 (i) 107, 1992.

48. E.J. Kanin, K.D. Davidson and S.R. Scheck, 'A Research Note on Male-Female Differentials in the Experience of Heterosexual Love', *The Journal of Sex Research* 6:64–72, (1970).
49. C.W. Hobart 'The Incidence of Romanticism During Courtship', *Social Forces* 36:364, (1958).
50. Zick Rubin, et al. In *Journal of Social Issues* 32:1 as reported in *A New Look at Love*, (1976)
51. R.J. Sternberg and S. Grajek, 'The Nature of Love', *Journal of Personality and Social Psychology* 47 (iii):12–29, (1984).
52. Daniel Goleman, 'New View of Fantasy: Much Is Found Perverse', *New York Times*, May 7, 1991.
53. R.J. Sternberg and M. Barnes 'Real and Ideal Others in Romantic Relationships: Is Four a Crowd?', *Journal of Personality and Social Psychology* 49:1586–1608, (1985).

About the Author

L eil Lowndes, internationally recognized communications expert, has presented programmes in practically every major U.S. city. She has coached Fortune 500 executives on interpersonal communications and has conducted communications seminars for the U.S. Peace Corps, foreign governments, and major corporations. She is the author of three books, including the top-selling *How to Talk to Anybody About Anything* (New York, Citadel Press, 1997).

Prior to her work in communications, Ms Lowndes was Founder and Director of The Project, a New York City-based not-for-profit organization that conducted relationship research and counselling. She is a member of the American Association of Sex Educators, Counsellors, and Therapists.

Based in New York City, the author has lectured at dozens of universities and colleges and has appeared on hundreds of television and radio programmes.